The SPAGHETTI GANG

Memories of a Crested Butte, Colorado
Coal Miner's Son

By Richard Guerrieri with daughter Cara Guerrieri

front: *Richard Guerrieri looking like a typical Spaghetti Gang kid. 1937, Crested Butte.*
back: *Richard's cousins Fortes and Gus Veltri in front of the CF&I tipple in the early 1930s. Crested Butte.*

Richard and Phyllis Guerrieri's cattle brand, –/– (Bar Slash Bar), marks the end of each chapter.

ISBN 978-0-9995450-3-4

Printed in the United States of America
First printing 2017

Richard Guerrieri and Cara Guerrieri
Gunnison, Colorado
SpaghettiGang@guerrieri.net
SpaghettiGang.com

Dear daughter, Cara. I can't imagine the untold hours you endured assembling this book. Through your determination and persistence, The Spaghetti Gang came into existence. Thank you for your patience and love for my story. May life treat you well.

Bless you, Dad

Dedication

This book is dedicated to all the immigrant families of my time and those who followed. They risked everything for freedom and prosperity. I am a proud grandson of immigrants. My life belongs to them.

The year was 1913. My grandma Rosaria Potestio Guerrieri and her son, four-year-old Gennaro (Jim), had returned to Italy from Crested Butte, Colorado in hopes of bringing Rosaria's oldest child, Teresa, to America. Thirteen years earlier Rosaria had come to America but, knowing that the United States did not allow immigrants with physical or mental deficits to enter, she had left Teresa, who had a cleft palate, back in Italy with relatives. More recent immigration policies had led Rosaria and her husband Gaspar to believe Teresa would at last be allowed to join the family in Crested Butte.

After Rosaria and Jim traveled from Crested Butte to Grimaldi, Italy to fetch Teresa, the three of them headed back across the Atlantic, arriving in New York just days before Christmas. At Ellis Island, Teresa was singled out for special review. They waited for three days, and on December 26, 1913 at 10:45 in the morning, immigration officials decided Teresa must leave the country immediately, all because of her deformity.

Rosaria crossed the Atlantic Ocean four times in one year, attempting to bring the whole family to the U.S. The S. S. Laura, above, almost sank on one of those trips.

Gaspar Guerrieri, my grandpa, a beloved and gentle man, came from Grimaldi, Italy to Crested Butte in 1891 at the age of 32.

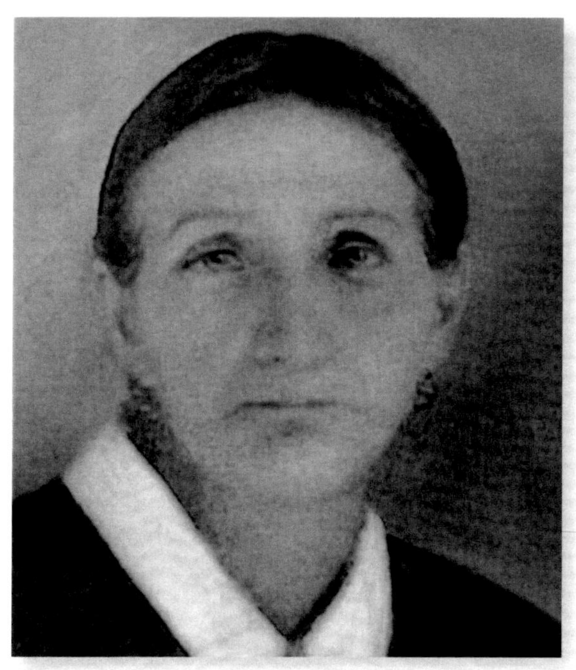

My resilient grandma, Rosaria Potestio Guerrieri, emigrated in 1900 from Grimaldi, Italy to Crested Butte to join her husband.

My maternal grandparents, Frances Mance Sneller and George E. Sneller (also spelled Sneler on some records) emigrated in 1893 from Croatia to Floresta, Colorado before moving to Crested Butte.

She boarded the S.S. Laura with Rosaria and Jim, bound once again for Italy. Rosaria sent the sad news to Gaspar. The Guerrieris had decided they could not live in America without their daughter, so Gaspar began preparing to leave their new life and return to Grimaldi, back to the life of grinding poverty they'd tried to escape.

Rosaria was 48 years old and for the eighth time she set about to bury one of her children, this time without her beloved and gentle Gaspar at her side. Only six of their fourteen children would live to adulthood.

Meanwhile, the S.S. Laura steamed east, and had almost reached Italy when it began taking on water. Rosaria and the children were stuck in the lowest level of the ship. As the water rose in the dank, crowded conditions, the wet, frightened passengers waited for ship's officers to come and help them. The officers did not arrive. Only one tiny, illiterate peasant woman, Rosaria, dared approach those in charge. She didn't speak the same language as the men, but she stood before them and insisted that those in steerage be brought to the deck. She gestured and gesticulated and didn't back down until everyone below, up to 1,500 passengers, were allowed above board.

The upper deck was treacherous as well. The ship took on huge waves that swept across the deck, washing all their belongings overboard except the clothes on their backs. Lifeboats were made ready but the ship did not sink. The S.S. Laura limped back to Naples, but by then many passengers, including Teresa, had become ill. Days later, Teresa died of double pneumonia. Rosaria was 48 years old and for the eighth time she set about to bury one of her children, this time without her beloved and gentle Gaspar at her side. Only six of their fourteen children would live to adulthood.

She spent the next six months in Italy before she and Jim boarded a ship back to America. It was her sixth and final trip across the Atlantic Ocean.

Back in Crested Butte, she picked up where she'd left off, as a healer and midwife who was known as "Grandma" not only to her grandchildren but also to everyone in town. Her grandson, Fortes Veltri, wrote in his memoir that she was "always there, always caring, lifting the load, filling my heart with courage and warmth." Her story is the story of our family, but it is also the story of all immigrants, and of America itself.

Table of Contents

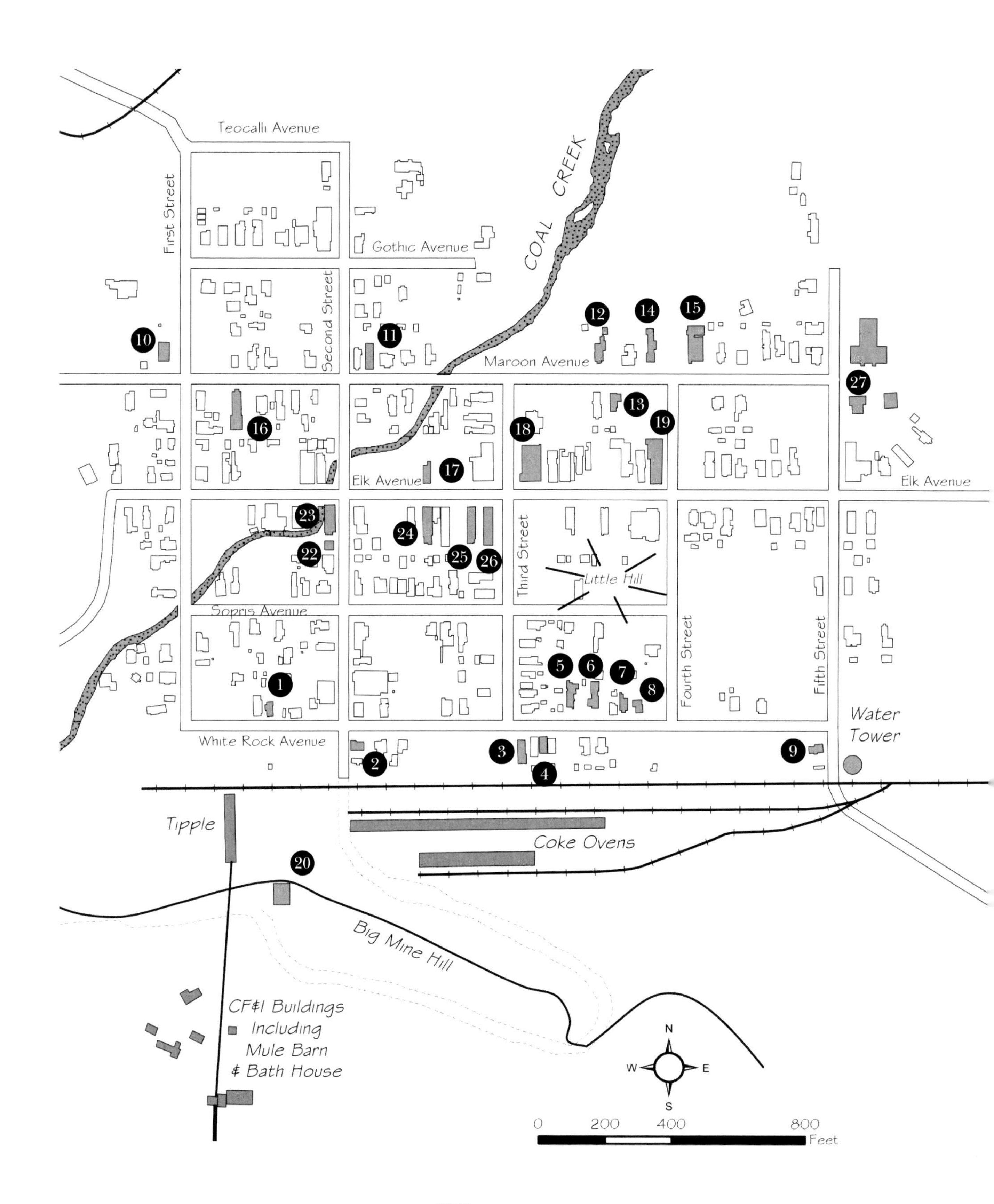

Teocalli Avenue
First Street
Gothic Avenue
COAL CREEK
Second Street
Maroon Avenue
Elk Avenue
Third Street
Little Hill
Sopris Avenue
Fourth Street
Fifth Street
Elk Avenue
White Rock Avenue
Water Tower
Tipple
Coke Ovens
Big Mine Hill
CF&I Buildings Including Mule Barn & Bath House
N
W
E
S
0
200
400
800
Feet
1
2
3
4
5
6
7
8
9
10
11
12
13
14
15
16
17
18
19
20
22
23
24
25
26
27

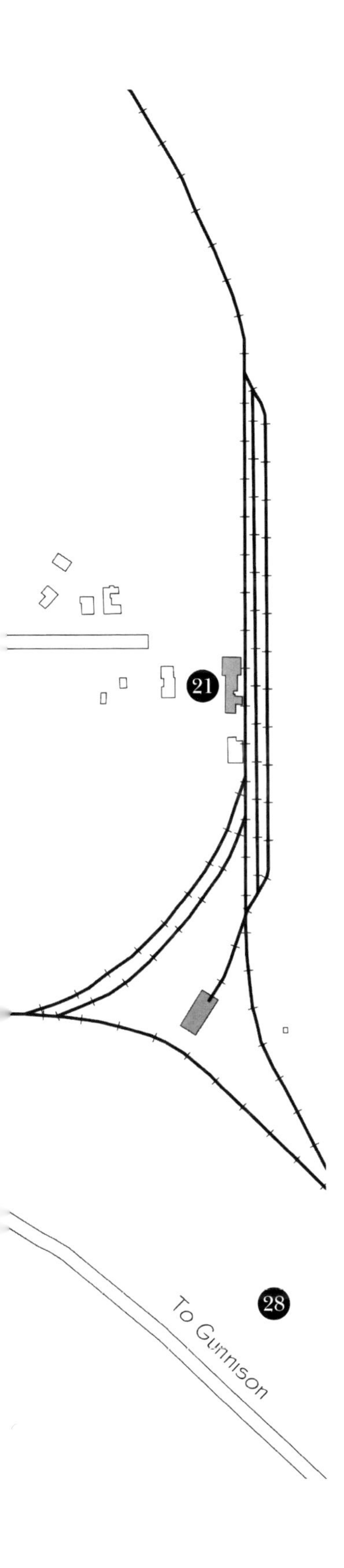

Town of Crested Butte, 1930s

1. 117 White Rock – George & Frances Sneller House
2. 202 White Rock – "A Time of Turmoil"
3. 302 White Rock – "The Twins and the Fancy Outhouse"
4. 306 White Rock – Giardino House
5. 311 White Rock – Gaspar & Rosaria Guerrieri House
6. 317 White Rock – Carricato House
7. 323 White Rock – Veltri House
8. 327 White Rock – Veltri House
9. 460 White Rock – Jim & Mary Guerrieri House "Funny in Retrospect"
10. 29 Maroon – Malensek House
11. 205 Maroon – Christoff House "War in the Attic"
12. 317 Maroon – Lunk House
13. 322 Maroon – "An Unusual Sex Ed Lesson"
14. 329 Maroon – Morgan House – "Flying Dots on the Page"
15. Protestant Church
16. Catholic Church "The Dreaded Catechism"
17. Mattivi's Bar "Beer Delivery Boy"
18. CF&I Company Store "Talk About Heaven"
19. Hardware Store
20. CF&I Office
21. D&RG Depot & Telegraph Office "Dot Dot Dash"
22. Jail
23. Town Hall
24. Princess Theater
25. Stefanic's Store "Beef Straight Off the Range"
26. Spehar's Store "Milk Delivery Boys"
27. Schools
28. Halazon Ranch "A Horse Named SOB"

Area Map of Crested Butte

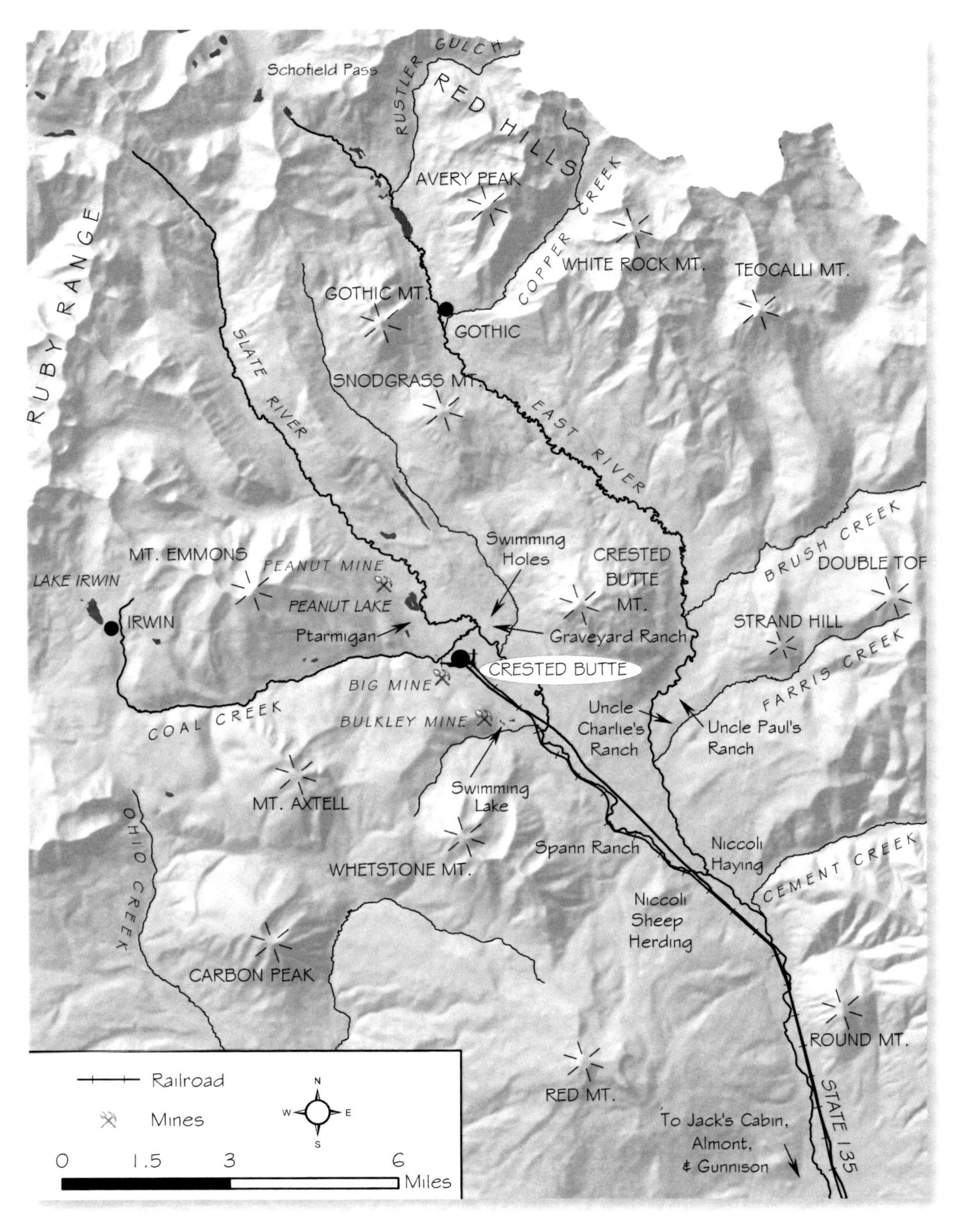

Forward—Writing with Dad

Dad handed me several spiral-ring notebooks, each line filled with his clear, graceful handwriting on both sides of each sheet. "See what you can do with this," he said. I should have known when he told me in the winter of 2016 that he was "doing a little writing while your mom swims," that it might be one of his typical understatements. Being a slow writer myself, I was stunned at the volume of his work. I don't know what prompted him, a life-long rancher, to take up pen and paper and fill notebooks with childhood memories. I do know that in their eighties both of my parents have turned to the arts to record and take stock of their lives. Mom paints charming and often humorous watercolor scenes from life on the ranch, and Dad writes.

Over the next months, he and I tackled the job of editing. He'd show up at my house unannounced, with a copy of the manuscript in hand. "Let's hit it," he'd say, settling himself onto my couch and placing his spittoon cup nearby.

I'd cancel whatever plans I had for the morning—when your source is eighty-five years old, you'd better take advantage of every moment. We struggled with wording and storytelling, and kept each other from sinking into that age-old writer's curse, self-doubt.

His original writing was stream-of-consciousness storytelling. He'd start a story about a childhood character, such as his cousin Jimmy Christoff, and out of the blue would be the sentence, "We still get a Christmas card from his daughter up in Idaho." Or a few paragraphs into an anecdote he'd remember part of an earlier story. "Back to that Uncle Paul story," he'd write.

Sometimes I pushed for details he either couldn't or wouldn't provide. One day as I drove him and Mom to their heart appointment in Grand Junction, I asked him to look at a chapter I'd edited. "I left it on the backseat next to you," I said.

After several minutes, he tapped one of the pages several times and said, "This here ain't right."

"Which part?" I turned on my right-hand blinker, heading toward Delta.

"Nora was a bay horse. My dad's mare was white," he said.

"Okay, that's an easy fix," I told him, then proceeded to suggest that he, "come up with a sentence about the look and feel of White Rock Avenue back when your dad and the men saddled up and rode to the mine each day."

"Well, I say right here it's a dirt street," he argued. "What more do you need?"

"Actually, there's a lot to describe—the color, smell, sound."

"Are you telling me readers are so dumb they can't picture a dirt street with horses going down it?" His tone bristled with disdain.

"Description would make the story richer." I eased into traffic.

Cara and Richard with an early draft of The Spaghetti Gang, June 2016.

"There ain't nothing more to say about a dirt street," he said, ending that discussion.

We were quiet for a few moments, and he moved on. "You don't need this here," he said, telling me to remove a sentence I'd added explaining the definition of a "cut proud" horse.

"But some people have no idea what that means," I said.

"Cut proud is cut proud. We can't go about explaining every damn thing."

And so it went, on the way to the appointment, on the way home, and week after week as we worked on his stories. I wanted more detail; he resisted. Sometimes I prevailed—in the end he did describe White Rock Avenue. Sometimes I didn't—the reader can look up cut proud.

Every so often, critical information came at unlikely moments. Over and over I asked him for the names of the kids in The Spaghetti Gang. For weeks, he simply couldn't remember and then one day he said, in reference to a different story, "That reminds me of the time Jiggy Vernon and I—."

"Wait. Who's Jiggy Vernon?"

"One of the Spaghetti Gang kids," he said, and my heart jumped a little.

Eventually he remembered not just Jiggy, but Frank Bruno, Gus Veltri, and Alberto. Names so perfect for a gang I still haven't stopped smiling.

Other times we'd get hung up on just a word or two.

"Dad," I said one time, "When you say you were amazed, can you describe your amazement? Did you raise your eyebrows, did your heart-rate speed up, your mouth fall open, or what?"

"Well, I was amazed. Like I said."

Fifteen minutes and much discussion later, he decided his eyes widened.

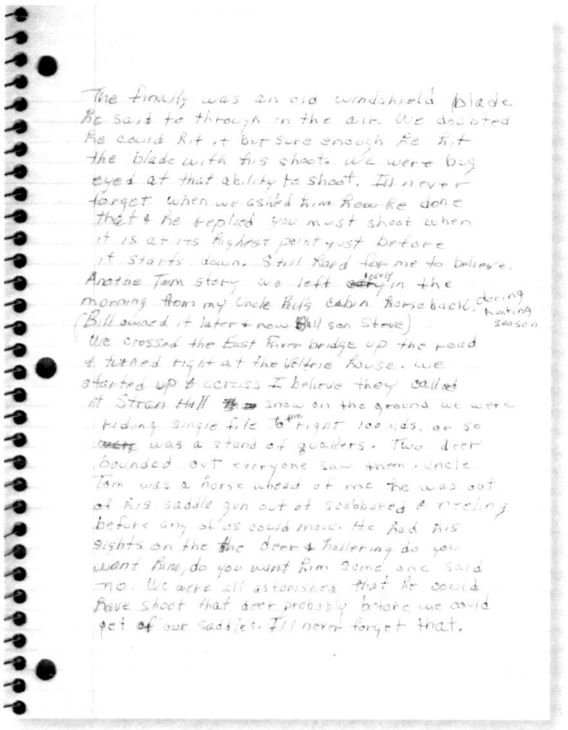

Original manuscript in Dad's handwriting.

Thinking we'd never get through a whole book at this rate, I said, "Dad, you know, this has to be a compromise. They say in a good compromise, neither party ends up entirely happy."

He folded his arms, tipped his head and squinted, as he does. "Well, in this compromise only one person is going to be unhappy, and it ain't gonna be me."

The stories that follow reflect a man I've known, loved, and admired my whole life, but whose childhood experiences until now were a blur. Working on this book with him not only put his youth into focus, but the hours we spent together also revealed levels of insight, humor, and humility in him I'd never fully grasped.

Many compromises and much aggravation and laughter later, this is our manuscript. As much as I love the tales that follow, for me, the experience of writing it together will always be greater than the sum of these words.

Cara Guerrieri
July 2017

Acknowledgements

Special thanks to Jenica Barrett, Richard's granddaughter, who turned the pages he wrote in a spiral notebook into an electronic document.

We appreciate the help of several generous community members. Nel Burkett at the Crested Butte Mountain Heritage Museum helped find photos and other historic data. Molly Minneman at the Town of Crested Butte shared detailed historical information about Crested Butte's old buildings and neighborhoods. Hilary Mayes turned hen-scratched drawings into professional, accurate maps. Kathy Amen, our brilliant designer, worked with us to get the look and feel we wanted in this book.

Sandra Cortner read several drafts. The value of her advice on organization, technical editing skills, and design cannot be overstated. Duane Vandenbusche, a long-time family friend, read the book and said, "include more photos," so we scoured the family archives one more time. Toni Todd added a little spit-shine and polish with her copy editing skills. We're grateful to Anne Hausler, a wonderful writer and friend, who always took our calls and offered her terrific insights.

Many extended family members shared photos that help tell this story, especially Brenda Mielke, Connie Guerrieri, Charles Guerrieri, Kathy Simillion, Patty Guerrieri Weihs, and Lee Spann. Many of the old pictures were unlabeled, and we did the best we could to recognize and identify the people in them. Any errors are ours alone.

Thank you to Mike Guerrieri, Max Guerrieri, and Ruth Guerrieri Barrett for hours of proof reading and final layout advice. Our entire family kept cheering us on. Their love and support made all the difference.

Introduction

The Spaghetti Gang is the delightful memoir of Richard Guerrieri, a coal miner's son who grew up in the rough mountain town of Crested Butte, Colorado. It is the story of Italian immigrant people and their lives during the Great Depression and World War II. Crested Butte was a coal town, dominated by the Colorado Fuel and Iron Company. It was a true American melting pot made up of immigrants from Ireland, Scotland, England, Wales, Italy and the Austro-Hungarian Empire.

Guerrieri's account of his boyhood is wildly entertaining. His stories feature ranching, coal mining, Catholicism, World War II, hunting, skiing, and many other activities involving a young boy. He recounts the customs of the Italians and other ethnic peoples of Crested Butte who made blood sausage, barbecued "whistle pigs," and got most of their food from deer, elk, and fish and from spectacular and well cared for gardens.

The Spaghetti Gang is filled with the nostalgia of a young boy growing up at a time when Crested Butte families had very little. Readers are treated to vignettes about "strap-on skis," "no bathing suits," "a horse named SOB," "the dreaded Catechism," and many other hilarious stories.

Crested Butte was a microcosm of coal towns in America during the dark days of the Great Depression. In 1952 the Crested Butte coal mine shut down and three years later, the railroad tracks were torn up. Crested Butte's population fell to 300, a near ghost town before its revival as a ski town in 1961. Guerrieri's account of his early life and his family's transition from coal mining in Crested Butte to ranching in Gunnison, Colorado, shows that amidst the economic woes of the time there was fun and adventure to be had. His stories read very well and are brilliantly written. They make up a great picture of days gone by.

The Spaghetti Gang tells a unique and heart-warming story of an ethnic coal town in American history. Crested Butte was, and still is, a great mountain town with a rich history. *The Spaghetti Gang* brings it to life.

Dr. Duane Vandenbusche
Professor of History, Western State Colorado University

The SPAGHETTI GANG

Chapter 1

Almost Across the Tracks

A pretty good view of White Rock Avenue (Spaghetti Avenue), the wide street with meandering tracks in the snow. 1930s. Courtesy of the Crested Butte Mountain Heritage Museum.

Spaghetti Avenue

I was born at home, straight into the hands of my grandmother, Rosaria Potestio Guerrieri. Grandma was a healer of sorts, and on occasion also a midwife, as she was on April 4, 1931, the day I was born. We lived in a simple wood-framed house on White Rock Avenue, in the coal-mining town of Crested Butte, Colorado.

By the time I arrived, Grandma was a widow. Her immigrant husband, Gaspar, had died several years prior, but not before they'd built a full life in America, surrounded by family and other folks from the old country. On our street, there were Croatians and Austrians, but mostly there were Italians, which is why instead of White Rock, folks called it Spaghetti Avenue.

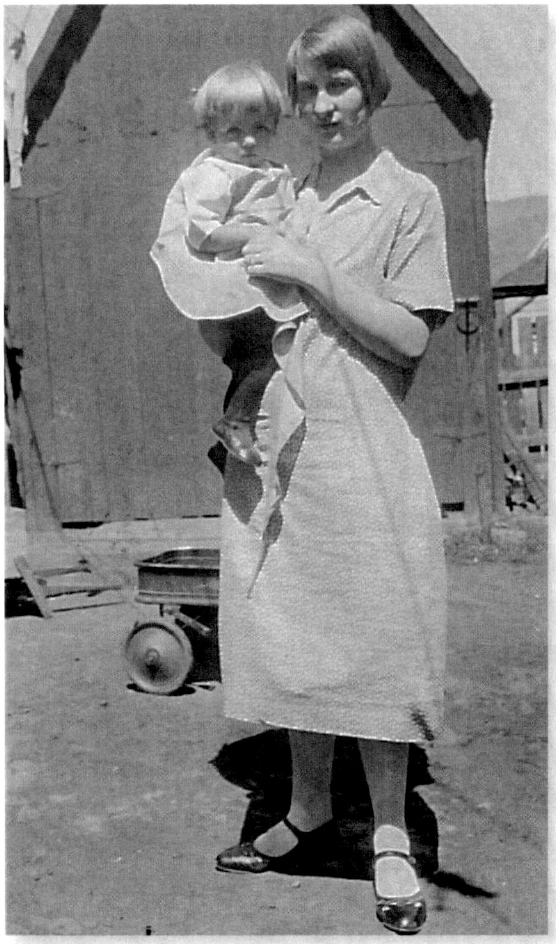

My mom and me in the back yard of Grandma's house on White Rock Avenue. 1933.

Next door to us was the Carricato family, who came from Calabria, the same region of Italy as the Guerrieris. A bright-eyed, musical family, they've been our neighbors in America for over a hundred years. The Charlie Veltri family was next to them, and on the opposite side of the street was my aunt Angelina Guerrieri, who was married to a different Veltri. Uncle Jim Guerrieri lived a few doors down near the coal train's water tank. The other close neighbors were the Giardinos and the Falsettos. The son of the Falsettos still lives in Gunnison and goes to the Young at Heart lunch with us.

Between White Rock Avenue and the rest of the town was a small rise, which we called Little Hill, on Fourth Street where Sopris Avenue comes in. A pretty cross stood on top of that hill, and in my memory, there was also a little chapel-type building there, in the same place where Queen of All Saints Church is now. Small of a rise as it was, Little Hill

My grandma Rosaria Guerrieri holding me. She was a respected midwife and healer. Crested Butte, 1932.

My folks and me, Crested Butte, 1934. Looks like we were dressed up for church.

nonetheless segregated those of us on White Rock from the rest of the town, almost as if we lived "across the tracks," as they say, but not because we were economically different than anybody else. Mostly it was because we were almost all family, spoke primarily Italian, and were a close-knit neighborhood.

Grandma was old and stooped over, like the bent cane she carried.

There was a yard out back of my grandma's house where the women kept some goats and a milk cow. They made their own goat cheese, cream for their coffee, and we drank the best milk in the world. My grandpa's old wood-fired brick bread oven still stood out in the yard. I grew up hearing stories about the bread he baked, the same as the heavy round loaves he'd grown up with in the old country. He'd make large batches and give it away up and down the street, to the Carricatos, Aunt Angelina, the Giardino brothers, and definitely to Uncle Jim's family. My grandfather was a generous guy, but so were the rest of the family and the neighborhood, too.

Grandma was old and stooped over, like the bent cane she carried. She never learned English, so I didn't understand much she said, but she and I got by.

The miners with aching shoulders were always coming to our house to ask if she'd massage their pain, which she always did, for free. One day my sister Pauline twisted her ankle and came home limping and crying. Grandma massaged Pauline's ankle and to this day Pauline claims that Grandma made her ankle feel better right away. "She was like a witch, kind of, the way she could make sore muscles feel better," Pauline says.

I was a skinny kid and was born with one testicle that was not in the sack, so when I was a little older, four or five years old, Grandma massaged it into place. It was not a pleasant experience exactly, but while she massaged she would sing in Italian. Beautiful, soft, melodies that made me comfortable and drowsy. Her hands were calloused from chopping wood, hauling coal, you name it, but when she began to work on that irregularity in my body, I didn't notice the roughness.

Every day she worked a little more and eventually she solved my problem.

She was a tough woman, never looked happy, and didn't smile, but she was a driven, spiritual healer who was held in high esteem in our little town.

Grandpa Gaspar Guerrieri in the early 1900s. He had a brick oven in the back yard and made big batches of "old country" bread.

I was born in this little house at 311 White Rock Avenue in 1931.Crested Butte, 2016.

The Twins and the Luxury Outhouse

Mom didn't know she was pregnant with twins until she was in labor. With my sisters, Pauline and Lucille, on White Rock Avenue. Crested Butte, 1935.

During her pregnancy with my twin sisters, Mom didn't go out of the house much. She had no idea she was having twins and being a private woman, she was ashamed of her enormous belly.

After a time, the family knew something about her pregnancy wasn't normal. She and my dad went to Salida, a big trip in those days, to see a doctor. At the hospital, the doctor examined her and then called in all the other physicians and nurses to see. Mom was mortified at all the commotion in her room. "I thought they were coming in to laugh at how big I was," she told us. "They didn't tell me I was having twins. I found out when I heard the doctors telling each other."

She stayed in Salida for the birth, and my sisters Lucille and Pauline were born in the hospital without the benefit of Grandma's midwife skills. Mom had the twins natural—I don't think there was even such a thing as a C-section back then around here, at least not that I ever heard of.

I have no idea how my folks managed to raise twins with all the other work they did, but I'm sure the extended family helped out. I don't remember any other twins being born in Crested Butte.

When the twins were still toddlers we moved up and across the street to a small house with a vacant lot out back, on the corner of White Rock and Second Avenue, the last house before the railroad tracks. Around that time, my Grandma sold her house and moved in with Uncle Jim's family.

My dad and his horse, Paddy. Such a splendid animal. The Old Rock Schoolhouse in Crested Butte is behind them. 1930s.

Our "new" house, which was not much better than a shack, truth be told, had a covered shed runway to the outhouse, which was a luxury compared to trooping through the snow. I really enjoyed using it, as it was the first time in my life I didn't have to run outside to go to the bathroom.

Behind the outhouse was a shed where my dad kept his horses. At that time Dad owned Paddy, a dark sorrel blood-red horse, splendidly proportioned, and Daisy, a black mare with a blaze face and with a few white spots.

Those horses, Daisy and Paddy, gave me my first sex education. I was young, not yet in school. One day I ventured back to the horse shed and Paddy was having his way with Daisy, probably cut proud. I couldn't believe what was going on there, but it was not the most memorable experience of living in that house.

A Time of Turmoil

One day Lucille, Pauline, and I were playing with coffee cans in the small kitchen. Seemed to me like we were kicking the cans and chasing them around the room. The lid of one of the cans came off and Lucille fell on the sharp edge of the can, which cut across half of her nose and her cheek. She was a tiny girl, just a toddler, but you wouldn't believe the blood. It was everywhere.

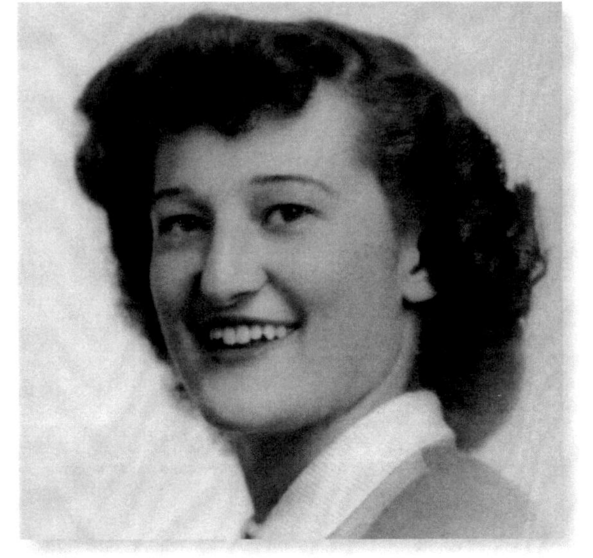

My sister Lucille recovered in spite of being stitched up by a drunk doctor. 1940s.

My mom came a-running and scooped Lu up and ran across the street to a wonderful lady, Mrs. Sedmak. Pauline and I didn't know what to do. We went out into the street and stood there scared and crying while total chaos took hold

A runaway team of horses split on either side of the electric poles on White Rock Avenue. My uncle Tom Sneller in front of one of the poles. Crested Butte, late 1920s.

around us. Neighbors running up the street, all kinds of hollering.

Someone got in touch with my dad at the mine—I can still see him coming down White Rock on Paddy, racing through the fog like a ghost, still dressed in his mine clothes, a sheepskin lined leather jacket and leather pants. Paddy was wringing wet and steaming from sweat after the four-mile run all the way from the Bulkley Mine.

By then the family had fetched Dr. Alford, who was a drunk. I don't know what kinda shape he was in that day, but he patched Lu up. She had an awful-looking bandage on her for some weeks, a sad-looking thing on a tiny girl, and we were in turmoil about it. After the bandage came off, she had ugly scars until later in life when she had cosmetic surgery. She ended up being a very pretty woman.

Lu's accident is etched in my mind like a carving in granite, solid and permanent. Some childhood memories are like that, and in my case, many of the most lasting recollections are scenes from White Rock Avenue.

Shredded Like a Snakeskin

One day while Lu was recuperating, the Colorado Fuel & Iron Company (CF&I) store delivery wagon rumbled up the street, pulled by a pretty, matched set of horses.

A delivery team braves the snow-covered streets of Crested Butte in February, 1909. Courtesy of the Pioneer Museum, Gunnison, Colorado.

The team was nowhere near as impressive as the four-horse hitch of pinto horses I liked to watch that belonged to old man Pobrik. I'd watched Pobrik pull a load of timber props to the Big Mine just a few days before, and I was mighty impressed. In my mind's eye, I can still see those amazing matched horses coming up the street, straining under the weight of the lumber they hauled. I kept an eye on those kinds of goings on, mostly because I was fascinated from an early age by animals, especially horses.

On the day the less impressive CF&I team made their trip up the street something or other spooked them and by God they bolted up the street, the delivery driver hollering and pulling on the reins. At first the team avoided the wooden electric posts halfway in the middle of the street and the iron light fixture posts that were smack in the middle of the intersections. When the runaways reached the intersection, the horses split one of them steel posts, each horse on the opposite side. The driver jumped clear as the leather harness shredded like a snake's old skin and the wagon jammed against the pipe. Wagon wheels tore off in a series of cracks and pops, splintering the wagon and sending groceries every which way.

Talk about excitement! Little old White Rock Avenue seemed to have its fair share. –/–

Chapter 2

A Few Memorable Characters

I've saved the quirt Joe braided for me for over 80 years. Last year I took it out of our saddle shed to show to our kids. Gunnison, 2016.

Joe Niccoli

Joe Niccoli lived with us when he was down on his luck, several years after this photo was taken in 1920. Crested Butte.

PLENTY OF TIMES MY MA WOULD FEED EXTRA MINERS who came around, and every once in a while, let them stay with us.

When our family friend, Joe Niccoli, came upon hard times, my folks put up a cot inside the doorway for him. He was a tall, thin, somber-faced fellow with kind eyes.

He worked at the mine with Dad and come evening, after supper, he and my dad sat around visiting. While they talked, Joe would get out strips of leather he kept in a bag under the cot and begin braiding them, knotting six strands of leather into all kinds of tack for horses. Watching Joe's hands pulling the leather strips this way and that into neat round braids was something I'd never seen before. He made me a rope halter and then a short quirt, which I still have down in the saddle shed.

Joe lived with us long enough to get back on his feet. Later in life he went on to marry a schoolteacher by the name of Hompton. They moved to Nebraska and had a family and prospered. After he died, his wife still corresponded off and on with my folks. They were lifelong acquaintances, and over the decades I've often remembered those peaceful nights when Joe braided and I watched in boyhood wonder. My folks, like Joe and most everybody in Crested Butte, were poor and striving for a better life, but as a kid I never thought of life beyond White Rock Avenue. Good or bad, there was always something happening.

Uncle Tom Sneller

My uncle Tom Sneller, unfortunately, was an unsettling presence in our lives. Too many times Uncle Tom would come staggering into our house barely able to stand after drinking at the bars. My folks would walk him up the street and deliver him back to his own house. Sometimes Dad, but most of the time Mom, took on the job of walking Uncle Tom up the street and seeing him safely into his own house. She'd give him a piece of her mind all the way. "Tommy," she'd say, "You've got to get a hold of yourself! Stop this drinking!" One thing that aggravated her to no end was that Uncle Tom never had a proper job like the other men in town. He preferred prospecting on his own, trapping for pelts, and living hand-to-mouth. From my bedroom window, I'd hear her as she walked him up the street, "Tommy, you need to get a job. They're hiring at the Big Mine."

Other times, when he wasn't drunk, she'd go at him again, hoping I'm sure to talk some sense into him, for he was an untold worry for the family.

The great anxiety he caused my folks was enormous and can't be overstated. I learned at an early age the toll on a family when alcohol takes over the life of someone you care about.

Drunk or sober, Uncle Tom never managed to take Mom's advice. He lived his life as an independent old cuss. A bachelor, he lived his whole life at 117 White Rock Avenue in the Sneller family home.

In his later years, his house got shabbier and shabbier. One time my mom and her sister, Aunt Kathryn, decided to clean it up for him. They snuck in one day when they thought he'd gone to check his trap-line. Well, he came back and found them mucking out his house and threw a royal fit. "Get the hell out of my house," he told them, "I like it the way it is."

The sisters never tried that stunt again.

Decades later, Uncle Tom finally straightened out and quit drinking, but the years of strife had taken its toll on his relationship with my mom. She never did let him cross the threshold of her house until she knew two things. First, that he wasn't drinking, and second, that he wasn't there for money. Oh, man did she read him the riot act. They'd go the rounds, those two, and I can tell you that growing up around all that agitation wasn't pleasant. There was too much drinking in Crested Butte in them days, and it affected many, many families.

Uncle Tom Sneller was quite the character and an untold worry to the family. Crested Butte, 1950s.

Big Nora

Lucky for me I was a kid who focused more on animals and kid stuff than adult worries. Big Nora, my uncle Jim's horse, fascinated me. Nora was a muscular horse, more refined than a workhorse but a large animal nonetheless. She had a set of hips on her that wouldn't quit and I believe if there was a Miss America of horses, she'd win.

During the winter, Crested Butte folks would put their cars up on blocks and park them for the season. There was no driving around town and back and forth to Gunnison and all over hell like there is now. Back then we had too much snow, too little plowing, and cars were not made for winter.

I was on hand to watch one day when a fellow on Sopris Avenue had his Ford stuck up to the running board.

Come spring, folks would be itching to get out their cars as soon as possible. Fairly often they'd get stuck in the muddy streets and driveways, at which point they'd get ahold of my uncle Jim to pull them out with his bay mare, Nora.

It was a big deal to get the car out in the spring. Winter seems to still have its grip on things in this late 1930s family photo. Uncle Charlie and Aunt Mary Guerrieri on the right. Crested Butte.

My uncle Jim Guerrieri on Big Nora in the 1930s. If there'd been a Miss America of horses, she would've won. Crested Butte.

Nora and her big hips were in demand and Uncle Jim, always a helpful guy, would saddle up whenever folks asked him to. He'd hook a big rope around the car bumper and he and Nora would start to pulling. There'd be more strain on that saddle horn than most single harness workhorses could muster. In fact, he had to buy a heavy-duty cinch because a regular cinch would break under Nora's power. I was on hand to watch one day when a fellow on Sopris Avenue had his Ford stuck up to the running board. Uncle Jim and Nora dug in, and the muscles in her hindquarters contracted so much her skin was bunched up tight and wrinkled, strange looking. Raw horsepower strained against the weight of the car and the soupy mud but, by God, Nora got the job done.

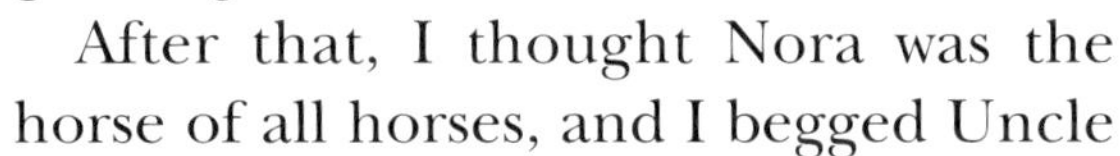

After that, I thought Nora was the horse of all horses, and I begged Uncle to let me ride her. A few days later I got my chance. Up and down White Rock Avenue I went while Uncle Jim kept his eye on me from his front porch. Nora had a calm temperament, and though I couldn't get her out of a walk, I was proud as a peacock, showing off, hoping to be noticed. After a few times up and down the street, I realized no one was paying the least attention to me. A kid riding a horse was the kind of thing that happened every day on our street. As much as I would've liked to have been watched and praised, the greater pleasure and the lifelong memory, is of my uncle thinking I was man enough to ride that grand animal. –/–

Chapter 3

The Graveyard Ranch

When we lived at the graveyard ranch, Dad rode to and from his work at the mine, five miles each way. Crested Butte, 1930s.

Almost Killed

I WAS NOT MORE THAN FOUR YEARS OLD when we left the cozy neighborhood on White Rock and moved to the Graveyard Ranch. The ranch got its nickname because of its location, just east of the Crested Butte cemetery, but for me its ominous name almost came true—twice.

Dad and my uncle Paul bought the ranch together, the sons of immigrants banding together to try to get ahead in America. It was their first try at ranching. The huge log home on the Graveyard Ranch had enough room for both families. The men built a partition so that Uncle Paul and Aunt Kathryn's family could live in the north half and we could live in the south. A door in the partition gave us the best of all worlds—easy access to each other and privacy, too.

An enormous barn on the ranch held harnesses, saddles, and horse stalls, all neat and organized, a reflection of the sentiment the family had toward animals. My dad, being a gentle, good man, was kind to his animals, always. He was also serious about the old country belief that at the stroke of midnight on the Eve of Epiphany, January 6, the animals would tell each other if their owner had been good to them. On that night, he believed the animals made a decision whether or not to work hard for him in the coming year. I'd go in that barn, kept clean and with fresh hay and rich grain all year long, and there was no doubt in my mind the animals said good things about Dad.

That cow started hell bent towards me, head down,
horns coming straight for me. I froze.

Between the house and barn was a shop-like building full of tools of all kinds, for carpentry, machinery, and leather. I wandered around that building and dreamed of the day I'd be a man and old enough to use them, not knowing then that for the rest of my life I would get great pleasure from working with large machinery, welding, and being an amateur mechanic.

The Graveyard Ranch supported our two families and a small herd of shorthorn cattle, maybe about thirty head. Shorthorns are a heavy, muscular breed with red hides. A unique breed, they're good for both milking and meat, so they were a logical choice for a small ranch.

One time when the men were working the cattle, I walked down to the corral and crawled through the gate. I got out into the corral and one of those shorthorns must have thought I was a dog—I was so small. That cow started hell bent towards me, head down, horns coming straight for me. I froze.

As luck would have it, my uncle Paul saw her coming. He busted his horse between me and the cow and headed her off. Then he jumped down out of his saddle and grabbed hold of me. He swatted my behind and told me in no uncertain words, "Don't you ever, EVER, come in this corral again. Do you hear me!" I left crying and just plain scared. I can still see that cow coming at me.

While they were running the ranch my dad and Uncle Paul both kept their jobs at the mine. From the Graveyard Ranch to the Bulkley Mine was about a ten-mile round trip by horseback every day. Can you imagine what they went through, riding horses in the winter with that far to go to the mine, loading coal all day, and also doing ranch chores morning, night, and weekends, feeding cattle in winter, haying in summer, irrigating, and doctoring?

A Wild Ride (Almost Killed Again)

I was four years old when my left leg got all cut up. Crested Butte, 1935.

The first year we lived at the Graveyard Ranch we had a big 4th of July barbecue, with all the family in attendance, which I can tell you meant a lot of people. Aunts, uncles, and cousins galore. Too many kids to keep an eye on.

My cousin Eva and I started messing around the cars, looking at them and such. We stopped at my uncle Jim's Chevy and she got in the driver's seat. "Pretend like you're a hitchhiker and jump on the running board," she said as she went about twisting the steering wheel this way and that, as if she was really driving. I went along with the game. Sure enough, that car jumped out of gear and started rolling down the hill.

There was an incline between the house and the barn and the car picked up speed before I could register what was happening. We were both petrified. I was too scared to jump off and tried to crawl into the car. I got my head and shoulder inside the window, hanging on for dear life as we barreled toward a horse-drawn sled maybe fifty feet ahead. The car hit that sled and veered to

Riding down this hill on the running board of the out-of-control car was a terrifying experience for a young boy. Eighty years later I still remember it like it was yesterday. Whetstone Mountain in the background. Crested Butte, 2016.

My cousin Eva Guerrieri several years after our accident. Gunnison, 1940s.

the right. The next obstacle was a barbed wire fence and below that, a big ditch filled with water. As the car traveled parallel to the fence, my legs still hung out the window. Closer and closer to the fence we got and in seconds, the barbed wire started riddling my legs with cuts.

I'm sure I was screaming to beat the band, and Eva, too. The car hit the ditch and stopped, and after that, I blanked out and don't know how everyone untangled us from that mess, but after a time they loaded me into another car. I bled all over the seats. They took me to Dr. Alford again, who was the CF&I company doctor. I don't know if he was sober that day.

He didn't stitch up my cuts like you'd expect. He took these metal clamps, like vise grips, and fastened them to my skin.

Afterwards, my folks put up a cot for me on the small porch on the south side of the house. The porch had a lot of windows that let the warm sun in and that's where I recuperated.

Any walking would have disrupted the clamps and torn up my legs again, so I was bed-bound until the cuts closed up. After a good long time, they drove me back to Doc Alford to get the clamps taken off. The cuts were deep and the doctor marginal, so I got a lot of scars from that experience.

The accident was scary for a little kid, and I can picture the incident in my mind like it was yesterday. Memory is a funny thing, though. Most of that day is crystal clear but I don't remember the pain at all.

After a few years, my folks sold the Graveyard Ranch to Chuck and Rena Halazon. Eventually young Joe Eccher and his sister inherited the place from their aunt Rena Halazon. When the development craze hit up in Crested Butte, they sold the ranch for big money.

None of the old buildings from the Graveyard Ranch are still standing. The old barn was there a few years back with a new house next to it. My wife Phyllis and I drove up to it because I would've loved to look inside that beautiful barn one more time but there was nobody home, so we didn't go in. Now it's been torn down. –/–

Chapter 4

To the Other Side of Town

The shed where we raised rabbits for eating, in the alley behind what is now the Crested Butte Mountain Heritage Museum. Crested Butte, 2016.

An Unusual Sex Ed Lesson

WE MOVED TO A NICE HOUSE MY FOLKS BOUGHT IN TOWN, 322 Maroon Avenue, across the alley from the Crested Butte Hardware, clear on the other side of town from White Rock. The hardware store, owned by a fella named Whalan, became the center of my universe.

Our house had a front room with a big window facing the street, a round coal heater stove in the middle living room, a back-door room, and a small kitchen. There was a cook stove with a copper water heater attached and a small bathroom directly behind the kitchen stove. Pipes led from the stove to the bathroom. In the mornings, I'd run downstairs to get dressed in the bathroom where it was cozy warm from the hot water tank. What an amenity!

The two bedrooms upstairs were not so cozy. For insulation, they were lined with newspaper. When we woke up on winter mornings, you could see your breath—talk about cold! The Maroon Avenue house was the nicest place I'd lived in my young life, but by today's standards it would be considered sub-standard.

I wondered about the buck's reaction but didn't dwell on it.
One more sex ed lesson, not exactly reassuring.

In the back yard, over towards the alley, we kept a half dozen or so doe rabbits in cages, and one buck. It was my job to feed and take care of those rabbits. I had one other chore, which was to haul enough buckets of coal into the house for heating, and I can tell you, the coal-hauling was easier than the rabbit chores.

Who knows what we fed the rabbits, probably grass clippings and the like. I don't remember that, but I do recall that there were water cups and little salt rings we hung from the cages. Every night in wintertime I'd empty the water because otherwise it would freeze and then I'd have to take the cups into the kitchen and wait until the damn ice melted.

I also had the chore of putting the buck in with the does for breeding purposes. On one occasion the doe must have been ready so the buck did his job. And then he fell completely backwards and lay there, stunned! I wondered about the buck's reaction but didn't dwell on it. One more sex ed lesson, not exactly reassuring.

For every doe, we had a box in her cage where she would give birth. When it came close to her time, she would begin to pull hair from herself to line the box. The baby rabbits would be born in a fluffy, warm nest.

When the baby rabbits were big enough, we had a pen to separate them, and my folks would check on them to determine when they were big enough to eat. My job was to kill and dress them. I would take a pop bottle, grab them by the hind legs, and hit them behind their heads to kill them. I was probably in the fifth or sixth grade, not very old. Looking back on it, killing those rabbits was a terrible event, I'm sure, but I never thought much about it at the time. It was a job to do.

Nowadays I hear about people not wanting to eat their pets, and I suppose the rabbits were our pets—they sure as hell weren't wild rabbits. I wonder now what a strange mindset I had at that age, because I so enjoyed eating my pet rabbits.

A Trick Horse

The lawn at the Maroon Avenue house was big and my dad bought a blaze-faced horse, a yearling, and kept her out there. We called her Ribbon and I'd go out on the lawn and brush and brush her until she shined. I decided to teach her to be a trick horse and do things like rear up when I raised my hands. I worked with her until she eventually learned how to do a few special things. I thought I was some kind of a horse trainer!

Ribbon wasn't part of our lives for a long time. There wasn't much sentiment when it came to making an extra buck; if my dad found a deal for making money he took it, and that was the case with Ribbon.

Back in them days, if you were hungry you raised and ate rabbits, and if you needed money, which we always did, you sold your horse for a profit. I've been fond of many animals over the course of my lifetime, but those early lessons of pragmatism when it comes to pets has stayed with me.

My dad, Gene Guerrieri, playing around on Ribbon, the trick horse. Crested Butte, 1930s.

My sisters, Lucille and Pauline, safe inside the fenced yard on Maroon Avenue. Crested Butte, 1940s.

As Brave as Tarzan

To keep Ribbon corralled and also to pen in my twin sisters, my folks put up a four-foot board fence on the backside of the yard next to the alley. I rolled a stump next to the fence so I could step on it and jump right over, but my sisters couldn't. That stump was pretty darn handy for me.

It was a cool thing to do, not to have to open the gate.

Occasionally my folks would allow me to go to a movie at the Princess Theater even though it was dark when I left the house. We had a bachelor living next door who had a couple dogs in his yard. The dogs barked like mad when I went past, and the bachelor was none too friendly, either. It took all the courage I had to walk up the dark alley past his place, all the while expecting his dog demons or him to come after me. It was less than a block down that alley until I reached the CF&I store where the streets were lit, but it was far enough so I was good and spooked.

On one occasion, I saw a Tarzan and Jane movie and I watched this half-naked man swing from trees, fighting nature's cruelties. There was nothing Tarzan couldn't conquer. That night when I walked back down the dark alley, I felt as brave as my new hero, Tarzan. The shadows, the bad-tempered bachelor, and the dogs were of no concern.

Back Problems and A Thin Wall

I was a stubborn kid, and a bit rebellious even as a youngster, often skipping piano lessons and the like. I don't suppose I was much different than most young boys but my mom had a short temper with me. When she got mad she'd whip me hard, which wasn't good. Looking back, I think her chronic hip problems contributed to her crankiness with me.

The pain in her hip got so bad, my dad eventually took her to Glenwood Springs to bathe in the hot mineral water for a month or so, hoping it would help. We were living at the time in the house on Maroon and I don't remember who took care of me and my sisters while my mom was gone.

Mom, Mary Sneller Guerrieri, raised a stubborn, rebellious son. Gunnison, late 1940s.

That year, on the 4th of July, Dad took me to Glenwood to see Mom. We stayed in a second story room in the Glenwood Hot Springs and watched the Independence Day parade from there. I remember the teams of horses hooked to fancy wagons. Those beautiful horses were all shined up. I was mesmerized. It was the first parade I can remember.

We also went to an amateur boxing match. The ring was four feet above the spectator seats and roped off. To a kid, it looked professional. Until then, I didn't realize hands could move so quick. Those boxers pummeled each other with lightning speed.

The cheering and the noise and shouting almost made you want to plug your ears. I don't recall who won. It didn't matter. That a poor kid like me got to attend a boxing match was the important thing, and even elevated my standing with the

I remember the Stimac boy boxing with his friend named Songer. Here he is years later at the Rosemont Café. Gunnison, 1940s.

Spaghetti Gang, at least for a little while. Boxing was a big deal in America back then, and we were all fascinated by those athletes.

When Dad finally brought Mom home from Glenwood, he built a special walled off area on the south side of the house. Mom lay on a cot naked in the sun every day for hours. She was a very, very tough person and began to get around as time went on. I have no doubt her problem was arthritis. Aunt Kathryn and Aunt Donna, her sisters, were all prone to arthritis, too.

One time after she got back from Glenwood I was walking by the Stimac yard, which was to the left of the Verzuh home on Maroon Avenue. One of the Stimac girls married Bob Robbins (a descendent of the Stevens family who owned a ranch that is under Blue Mesa, now called Stevens Point). Bob and his wife are both deceased. The other Stimac girl married a Ruggera and I think they are alive and still live in Crested Butte. Anyway, the day I walked by, the Stimac kid and another fellow by the name of Songer had their shirts off and were bare-fist boxing. When the fight first started, they didn't hit hard, just tapping to start. Then they moved on to harder punches. I could hear them smack, smack as they beat up on one another. It had to hurt. Eventually they got exhausted and quit. Afterwards they were still the best of buddies, which amazed me, as I figured they had to be pretty mad at one another to beat on each other like that.

In the family tradition, I suppose, I also had trouble later on, as a teenager, with pain in my hips. It got so bad that my folks decided I needed to see a chiropractor. So, I went to the chiropractor's office and he started fussing with me, measuring one thing and another.

There was also a fellow in the next room, a miner. After I was measured, the chiro left my room and went to the miner. The walls between the rooms were thin. The chiro would say something and shortly thereafter that miner would scream. A minute later, same thing over again. More screaming. By the time the chiro came back to me the fellow in the next room was in such pain he was howling.

I was ready to bolt when the chiro entered my room and announced, "Richard, you've got one leg shorter than the other, but I can help you out. Make an appointment for next week and we'll get started."

I'd heard enough of that miner hollering. That was it for me and chiropractors. I never went back to one, not then, not ever.

Rudy The Hound

Once we left the Graveyard Ranch and moved onto Maroon, we had new neighbors, too. Up to then my life had been dominated by extended family, living all up and down the street on White Rock Avenue, and in the same house as us at the ranch. But on Maroon Avenue, my world expanded.

Rudy always had a half dozen or so cow-dogs with him for the ride, and he'd let those dogs push the cattle hard.

Rudolph J. Malensek, 1942. Courtesy of Wes Bailey, V.F.W. Post 4665.

Just up the street from us lived the Malensek family. All winter long Rudy Malensek would ride his Morgan stud horse past our house to get to his ranch to feed his cows. That ranch is now the Crested Butte ski area. Rudy wore so many clothes you could barely see his face. I'll never forget that Morgan horse, which was a beautiful animal.

That was before Rudy enlisted in the army in 1942. He served for three years until the end of the war. He rarely spoke of that time to me, even though he

Matt Malensek, John Malensek, my dad, and Rudy Malensek at a pig roast at our Mill Creek ranch (Gunnison) in the 1970s. The Malenseks were our neighbors and friends in the early days in Crested Butte and after we all moved to Gunnison.

became a lifelong friend. When he sold his Crested Butte ranch, he and his brother Matt, who married sisters (Ann and Margaret Mihelich), bought a place down on the Lost Canyon Road in Gunnison. It just so happened that I ended up ranching nearby.

Long ranching hours don't allow much time for socializing, but from time to time on my way to check the Gunnison River headgate, I'd stop in to say hello to Rudy, Matt and their wives. Without fail, they were gracious hosts to an unannounced visitor, and before I knew it there'd be a glass of wine in front of me. We'd sit around talking about ranching and the like. The entire Malensek family had a particular rhythm and lilt to their speech, a leftover bit of accent from their native Slovenia. There was something about their way of speaking that made one think there was a smile or a bit of humor behind every word. I never liked wine, and on any other occasion I would turn down a glass, but in the company of the Malenseks it tasted just right. You'd think the wine might be something special, but it was just a bottle of Mogan David they bought in town, proving that good camaraderie improves the taste of most anything.

The old-time ranchers had a nickname for Rudy. My father-in-law, Aubrey Spann, told me how the moniker "Rudy the Hound," came about. When Rudy was young he was a regular cowhand and he hired on for the big cattle drives of the East Side Cattlemen's Association, a group of ranchers that pooled their stock together for grazing on federal lands. At that time, back in the 1930s and '40s, the association herded upwards of two thousand head of cattle along Highway 135 twenty miles from high up on Red Mountain to Gothic each July. Rudy always had a half dozen or so cow-dogs with him for the ride, and he'd let those dogs push the cattle hard. Now, if you push the back of a herd too much, you're bound to force a few of 'em through the fence, especially when calves are involved. Now, after a few times of Rudy's dogs forcing cows and calves through the fence, the ranchers told Rudy, "You gotta call off them dogs." Oh, did those ranchers love to banter back and forth, and they gave Rudy a good deal of grief, threatening to make him fix the fences if the cows went through. After that threat "Rudy The Hound" kept his dogs in check and they all got a good kick out of Rudy's nickname.

Of course, as a kid, my focus was on admiring Rudy's horse, never imagining how life would progress to the point that I'd be neighbors and friends with Rudy until he died, just a few years back. The future, as far as I was concerned back then, only extended to what kind of escapades and fun my friends and I would have that day. –/–

Chapter 5

Hot Summer Days with The Spaghetti Gang

That looks kinda like me on the right, but with twenty-four first cousins and no label on the old family photo, who knows? The No Trespassing sign seems fitting for the ornery Spaghetti Gang. Crested Butte, 1930s.

Crabby Old Man at the Lake

A BUNCH OF US KIDS, MOSTLY ITALIANS, hung around together and got nicknamed "The Spaghetti Gang," for obvious reasons. We weren't that tough, mostly a bunch of scrawny kids knocking around. We didn't have any rival gangs, though for a time we were a little intimidated by the older guys in town. Then a kid named Alberto, twice as big as the rest of us, joined the gang. After that, we weren't worried about the older boys. We loved Alberto.

We were nothing like gangs nowadays. If you wanted to join the Spaghetti Gang all you had to do was hang around with us. There was sure as hell no initiation and no qualifications needed to belong. Me, Jiggy Vernon, Frank Bruno, and Gus Veltri were regulars in the Spaghetti Gang, but others came and went. We weren't into doing bad things, but we were rascals.

When you're a kid in Crested Butte, hot summer days are meant for fishing and wading. I believe that's my mom in the middle with her brothers Tom Sneller (left) and George Sneller (right). Crested Butte, 1916.

During gardening season, one pastime at night for the Spaghetti Gang was sneaking around town and grabbing a little produce, like carrots and turnips or radishes (my favorite), then dashing off to eat them. We thought we were really something! Most of the gardens around town were pretty well fenced off, not to keep the deer out, but to deter the Spaghetti Gang.

An old guy near the church had the best garden and grew terrific turnips. We got into his garden quite a bit until he got kinda mean and fenced it real tight. The Spaghetti Gang, we were ornery, but never did nothing serious, though it would've been serious if my ma had known about it. Hard as she worked to put good food on the table, she woulda whipped me fierce if she'd known I was out stealing food just for fun.

Our antics were more mischievous than illegal, and oh, did we love a challenge!

On hot days, a trip to the swimming hole on the first hill going south out of Crested Butte fit the bill. A crabby old man lived up there on the right and just behind his house was a natural lake. Trespassers were not allowed, especially a bunch of ornery Italian kids, so it naturally became an appealing adventure for the Spaghetti Gang.

One hot summer afternoon, we snuck around the backside of the lake (which was a long walk from town), hoping the old cuss couldn't see us from his house. We made the long trek and we didn't get caught. Our success should have made the swim extra fun. Instead, we were all on edge, scared to death he'd see us. What should have been a relaxing swim was tense and fearful. After paddling around for a few minutes I was ready to be done. I floated toward the bank and scraped my belly on the gravel, which stung. Sometimes, it just doesn't pay to sneak around. That's about all I got out of that experience.

No Bathing Suits

An easier place to take a swim on hot days, because it didn't involve trespassing, was in Coal Creek. The best swimming hole on the creek was at a bend in the river across from the dumps. We'd stop at the dumps on the way to the creek and grab some wood or an old tire. The gang had a rule: bring something to burn or you can't swim.

Even though the river bend was fairly close to the road with only a barbed-wire fence separating the road from the river, we'd swim naked. Very few cars came by, but if one did, we'd turn our backsides to the road or jump back in the creek.

We swam off and on during the week all summer long, and the water never warmed up. We'd swim until we were shivering and almost numb, jump out and head for the fire, our skin colored red, and shaking like leaves in the wind until we warmed up.

One day we were hanging around the fire with two or three older boys, maybe sixteen or seventeen years old. All of us were stark naked, when here came a car, traveling real slow up the road. We looked at that old car and every one of us knew it was the old lady from the depot.

She came around the corner and about the time her car was straight across from us, most of us turned our backs, but the older boys, well, they turned to face her and started fondling themselves. That poor old lady was looking so hard at their antics, she drove off the road into the barrow pit. Luckily, she made it back onto the road without much trouble, and there were only a few barbed wire scratches on her paint job. We laughed till we darn near split, but later I realized it was kind of a cruel joke.

Man, woman or otherwise, you never get too old to look.

The gang had a rule: bring something to burn or you can't swim. Peter and Emil Spritzer, Crested Butte, 1923.

Big Mine Bathhouse

On days that weren't so hot, we'd head out from town toward the Big Mine bathhouse, which was at the top of the hill, around 150 stair-steps. From the bottom, it looked like the stairs went straight up at a ninety-degree angle. It was a daunting climb, but not for a gang of kids with a purpose. We'd take after them steps like conquerors, but by the time we got halfway up where there was a little landing, us heroes needed a rest.

Even Jiggy, a nervous jumpy kinda fellow, had to catch his breath. The last seventy-five steps were a slog and afterward we'd emerge from the stairway where I suppose the view was fantastic, but we never noticed. The mountains in front of us meant home, nothing more. We'd seen the views of Crested Butte Mountain, the Gothic and East River valleys, and up toward Peanut Lake every day of our young lives. Marveling at them was not something we did.

The Big Mine had an enormous shop with a lot of buildings surrounding the bottom of the mine and we still had to get around them without being seen. The workers wouldn't have taken kindly to a bunch of hooligans traipsing through.

This miner's bathhouse looks almost exactly like the bathhouse at the Big Mine in Crested Butte. National Park Service.

First, we'd creep around the huge two-story mule barn. The barn had stalls on the first floor and hay on the second floor. A ramp on each end made it so local ranchers could drive their teams of horses pulling wagons loaded with hay up one ramp, unload the hay, cross the barn, and drive out using the ramp at the other end. A set of scales weighed the loads before the wagons unloaded. The Big Mine needed a tremendous amount of hay for the fifty or more mules they used in the mine.

We'd skirt the barn and head around the fenced mule lot and past a big, warm spring, which ran through the mule corral and down into Coal Creek or wherever it went. The steam coming off

Left to right, my grandpa Gaspar Guerrieri, Joe Niccoli, Bill Hamilton, and two other miners by the name of Rozman and Mosher. Crested Butte, 1920.

the year-round spring had a sulfur smell, like other hot springs. If the gang made it beyond the spring without being caught, we'd crawl through a wide spot under the fence and we were home free.

To me it was as if those clothes were ghost people, empty likenesses of the hardworking men laboring underground in the mountain.

The bathhouse was about 150 to 200 feet long and 150 feet wide. The shower room had upwards of fifty showerheads to handle the needs of the mine's four hundred employees. The room was also clean as a whistle, the opposite of what you'd think with all the miners rinsing off black coal dust. The cement floors were painted gray with not a spot of black on them.

In the main changing area, a full-length bench stretched all the way down the side of the building, long enough for dozens of men to sit and dress at once. We'd

If the Spaghetti Gang made it as far as the CF&I mule barn without getting caught, we were almost home free. Courtesy of the Crested Butte Mountain Heritage Museum.

undress there and go stand under the big showerheads, seemed like forever, with endless hot water spraying down on our heads. None of us had showers at home—my ma heated water with the coal cook stove for the tepid baths me and my sisters took, one after another in the same water. But at the bathhouse, if we had everything timed right, we could stand there a long, long time before the miners got off shift.

We'd stay as long as we dared, then dry off in a hurry and pull on our overalls. Above us in that tall-ceilinged bathhouse hung rows and rows of miners' clothes. Clips attached to chains hoisted each man's clean clothes up out of the way, clear up by the rafters. At the end of his shift, the miner would do the same thing in reverse, running his clean clothes down and dirty mine clothes up on his own clip. Each chain had a number on it, so miners could identify their own clothes. The mine was at full production, which meant a lot of chains. To me it was as if those clothes were ghost people, empty likenesses of the hardworking men laboring underground in the mountain. An eerie sight.

We were intruders, and an ornery, curious bunch, but we had enormous respect for those men and one thing we never did was mess with those chains or the clothes. Instead, we knelt down, slipped on our lace-up boots, and hustled back to town and to the lively adventures of the Spaghetti Gang. –/–

Chapter 6

Food on the Table, Booze from the Bar

Every afternoon I got sent to the saloon with a bucket to fetch beer for my grandparents. I wasn't much older than the kid in the picture. Courtesy of the Crested Butte Mountain Heritage Museum.

When it came to cutting up a pig, the old timers sure knew what they were doing. My cousin Genevieve Christoff, Uncle Charlie Guerrieri, my dad Gene Guerrieri, Rose Guerrieri Carricato, Uncle Paul Guerrieri, Aunt Kathryn Guerrieri. Crested Butte, 1942.

Always Boiling Something

Everywhere we lived, I remember my mom working hard to can food for the long winter. She kept an old cook stove boiling all fall with fruits and vegetables for canning. Like everybody else, she had a big garden, and grew potatoes, turnips, carrots, and cabbage.

She made her own sauerkraut, just like they did in the old country back in Croatia, storing it in big wooden barrels. We ate sauerkraut at almost every supper, along with wild game meat and potatoes. We didn't eat fancy, but always had coffee and eggs for breakfast, and peanut butter and jam for noon lunches.

One good thing was that we never had to haul water for cooking. Even in the years we didn't have indoor toilets we did have running water. In winter, we'd leave the faucet turned on overnight to keep the pipes from freezing. Mom put an old sock over the faucet to mute the noise of that running water so we could sleep better.

Blood Sausage

Besides canning the vegetables we grew and the fruit the women of Crested Butte picked in Paonia, our family cured our own meat. A lot of it was sausage. Sausage making for a bunch of Italians is quite the deal, and started with buying some weaner pigs in the spring. The pigs couldn't be kept in town too easy so the families found ranchers to leave them with all summer. Since all the ranchers back then had a milk cow or two, they had plenty of leftover whey from making cottage and ricotta cheese to feed the pigs. A month before the butchering, the ranchers would grain the pigs, too, so that by fall those pigs would weigh about 250 pounds, no problem.

On butchering weekends Dad, Mom, members of the Guerrieri, Niccoli, Rozman, and Veltri families got together to slaughter the hogs. Me and my sisters and all the other kids trotted along, too. Usually our pigs were kept at the Sid Niccoli ranch, so that's where we went for butchering.

First thing to do was build a fire underneath a couple of metal half-barrels with legs standing two to three feet off the ground. The barrels were filled with water and there'd be a large wooden table close by.

A few of the men would drag a squealing pig next to the fire, where they'd shoot it in the head. Oh, what a painful racket them pigs made just before they got shot.

The dead pig was hoisted immediately up a tri-pod scaffold using a rope and pulleys. Someone would stick the pig in the neck with a knife after hanging it up and here came the women, scurrying in with buckets to catch the blood for making blood sausage. Blood gushed out for several minutes, all of it saved.

When the pig was pretty well bled out, the carcass got dropped into the boiling water, which was mixed with ashes to help loosen the hair. As soon as the hair started to slip, the men lifted the pig out of the water and moved it to a wooden table. That's where the real work started.

The women of Crested Butte used every part of a pig, but I could never stomach the pickled feet. My grandma Sneller. Crested Butte, 1930s.

Everyone had a big sharp knife and took turns scraping the hair off. All around the table they'd work like mad to get every hair, and by the time they were done, the hog would be slick, not one hair left, even on its nose or anywhere.

Then back to the scaffold that pig went and was raised up high, to be dressed out. Here came the women again with buckets, this time for saving the heart, the liver and all the intestines from the pig. When that was done, they covered the pig with blankets and loaded it into the back of a pickup truck and headed for my grandma Sneller's house.

What a scene in the Sneller dining room. Me and my sisters watched the whole goings on and tried to stay out of the way, but curiosity got the best of us now and again and we'd get hollered at for being too close. Grandma, Aunt Kathryn, Aunt Donna, and Mom cut the hams, the ribs, and the chops off the carcass. All those parts were for smoking. Anything left that couldn't be smoked got made into sausage. The feet they pickled, which was the only thing they made out of the pig that I truly hated.

The sausage making, now, that was quite the deal. The intestines got washed until there was nothing left but the casing. The scraps of meat, the spices, and the pork fat, got put into a big hand grinder that had a round metal tube about eight inches long sticking out of it. A piece of the clean pig gut got pushed onto the outside of that tube. One end of the gut was tied in a knot, and the women would go about pushing the meat into the grinder and out the tube. The ground-up concoction filled the intestine and when about five inches of casing was crammed full, the women tied a string around it, then pushed more meat. This continued until there was a string of sausages two or three feet long, just the right length for hanging in the smoke house.

In our family, we made two kinds of sausage: a spicy kielbasa with caraway seeds in it, a recipe from my mom's side of the family, and old country blood sausage from the Italians, which I loved. They made blood sausage by mixing the fresh pig blood they'd collected in a big vat with rice and spices where the mixture sat until the rice absorbed the blood and thickened. Then my ma and the women pushed that blood and rice mixture through the grinder and into the intestines, too.

We'd carry the strips of links to the smoke house, behind my grandparents' house in the yard. All the hams, ribs, and sausages got hung up high in the smoke house, probably about 15 feet off the ground. Underneath the sausages, on the ground, Grandpa Sneller built the fire. He kept it small and smoky, just right so the hot smoke cured the meat perfectly. Those old country people had the whole system figured out and down to a T.

On pig-butchering weekends, houses all over town were as busy processing the meat as ours. For several weekends in a row, folks and neighbors gathered up to butcher at various ranches. That way all the families had help with the hard work of slaughtering the pigs.

In those days, folks didn't worry about diseases from the blood or the meat the way we do now. All I cared about was how good that blood sausage was gonna taste. The women knew how to make sure the pork was clean and cured properly, and I didn't think to question it. My mouth still waters thinking of the blood sausage from those days.

Beef Straight Off the Range

One day I was walking up the alley behind Stefanic's grocery store and there was a truck backed up to the store. On the bed of the truck was a very large beef carcass, skinned and dressed. I stopped to watch while Tony Stefanic rolled a winch above the cow, hooked it up to the single-tree attached to the hind legs, and hoisted the beef up and onto a rail leading into the store.

1930s cattle drive from Red Mountain to Crested Butte and Gothic. Old man Stefanic often bought cattle on-the-hoof to butcher and sell at their store on Elk Avenue.

We ate wild game year-round. In 1938, a couple of deer hang in the back yard. My cousin Charlotte Guerrieri (left), sister Lucille (middle) and cousin Anton "Christy" Christoff (right). Crested Butte.

I always knew folks bought fresh beef at Stefanic's place, but I didn't know it was that fresh. I only found out later that Tony was known to buy fat heifers directly from nearby ranchers, often from Virgil Spann, whose ranch wasn't too far out of town. Sometimes he'd even show up at the fall roundup in Gothic to pick out a critter straight off the summer range.

People went into Stefanic's every day to buy fresh meat, and I never heard of anybody getting sick from bad meat so Tony must've kept a clean butchering operation. In those days, the store could sell the butchered beef directly to customers without any inspectors.

Burning the Evidence

One day an officer from the Game and Fish came around trying to catch our neighbor, Tony, for poaching. It was not an unusual thing in those days to hunt illegally, so it wasn't hard to figure out why the officer was parked outside Tony's place. Everyone on the street knew what was happening.

Now, it just so happened that my uncle Tom had dropped by that morning with the hindquarter of a deer he'd killed out of season. What if the Game and Fish stopped by our house? My mom panicked. She banked up the fire in the coal heater in the front room until it was very hot and threw in the entire hindquarter. The meat started to cook and you could see it in there popping and burning. What a sight! An entire hindquarter cooked at once!

That burning meat got to stinking so bad that me and my sisters went to the front yard, thinking we'd avoid the smell. Outside, where the black smoke rose from the chimney, the smell was even worse than inside the house. Everyone knew the stink of burnt meat, including the game warden, and we were scared to death that the officer was gonna come by and take Mom away for illegal activities, but neither the neighbor Tony nor my mom were hauled away to jail.

Beer Delivery Boy

Every afternoon I had an unpleasant job to do for my Sneller grandparents. I'd stop by their house and they'd hand me an empty half-gallon pail and some coins. My chore was to walk down to Mattivi's bar on Elk Avenue and get the pail filled with beer and return it to my grandparents.

Some older fellows horsing around and drinking in the late 1920s in Crested Butte. Left to right: first three unknown, Tony Mihelich, Tony Kapushion, my uncle George Sneller, Joe Saya, Joe Carricato, unknown.

Every afternoon my chore was to bring beer to my grandparents, Francis Mance Sneller and George Sneller. Crested Butte, 1930s.

A little kid walking into a bar to buy alcohol wasn't illegal in them days, but it wasn't normal either. You'd think everybody in the bar would look over at me. Here was this skinny, raggedy kid in worn-out overalls with a pail, a bit of money, and hardly tall enough to set the pail on the bar. If you didn't know better, you could've mistaken me for a vagrant orphan, and a drunk at that! It always made me uneasy, and I worried what I'd do if someone tried to talk to me, but I was a regular, so the men on stools at the bar and others at the tables drinking didn't pay much attention.

After I dropped it off to them, I hightailed it out of there, never hanging around while they drank their beer.

With the beer bucket full, I'd make sure the latch on the lid was tight and I'd lug it back the three blocks to my grandparents. After I dropped it off to them, I hightailed it out of there, never hanging around while they drank their beer. Not once. I'd been around enough drunks, even at a young age, to know I didn't want anything to do with that business.

I'd head on home or out to play marbles with the gang. It was a strange errand for a little kid, especially by today's standards.

Alcoholism is a bad deal and was prevalent in Crested Butte, as it was in most mining towns. All around me were examples of how alcohol destroys family. Sometimes the situations were amusing, or would have been if it hadn't involved real people.

I remember a small restaurant on Elk Avenue that was owned by a husband and wife. She did the cooking, and was a very tiny and wiry lady. Her husband was very heavy and didn't do much work, just stayed in that dark restaurant drinking his life away. Folks said he kept an eye on the cash register and spent all their money on booze. It didn't matter how hard she worked or how much money the restaurant made, with him in charge of the finances, the family was always broke. It was a situation that was true for too many families in those days. I was lucky that my mom and dad didn't drink a drop, which made my life a little more carefree than some of my friends. –/–

Chapter 7

The Spaghetti Gang Wanders the Streets

An earlier generation of Spaghetti Gang kids, my uncles Tony, Tom, and George Sneller. Crested Butte, 1918.

Hoops, Hopscotch, and Such

I CAN'T RECALL EVER TELLING MY MA WHERE I WAS GOING when I left the house each afternoon to play with my friends. None of the parents wondered where their kids had gone off to. The whole town watched out for one another so we were free to do as we pleased. Sort of.

If we did something wrong, you could bet somebody would dash to our moms and let them know. Then the "blank" would hit the fan. Back then, if you dropped a dime out of your pocket on Elk Avenue, folks on White Rock would know about it before it hit the ground.

We'd use old metal wheels, smaller than this one and without the spokes, for playing hoops. Annie Perko, Crested Butte, 1920.

Nowadays kids have organized things to do, but we just wandered the streets looking for entertainment. To make rambling around town a little more fun we invented "hoops," which involved finding an old steel wagon rim with no spokes from the dumps. The lighter in weight it was, the better. The rims we liked were maybe two to three feet high. We'd build a "U" and a handle from heavy wire and using the handle, we'd push those rims around town, balancing them in front of us with the handle, wherever we went. It was quite a challenge to roll those rims ahead of you and keep control over the uneven dirt terrain.

Of course, hoops didn't keep us occupied all the time, so we played a lot of hopscotch, a game nobody seems to play anymore. We spent hours drawing out complicated hopscotch markings in the dirt, and jumping square to square until we were plumb wore out.

Along about evening, or sometimes in the late afternoon, we'd play with pistols

I found a few of those old metal hoops on our ranch. Gunnison, 2017.

and rifles we made from crate lumber. I like to think we made some pretty sophisticated rifles, with barrels a couple feet long, notches for the ammo (thick inner tube bands), and a string underneath that released the shot. We could shoot three of four of those bands at once with a rifle, but the pistols we made would only shoot one band. The release for the pistol ammo was a clothespin.

We'd cart our firearms over to a dilapidated shed behind the Battiste family house across from the hardware store, and play cops and robbers. The shed had runways, rooms, and a lot of places to hide both inside and out in the yard. We entertained ourselves for hours, hiding from the "cops" and shooting each other with bands. Why no one ever got shot in the eye with one of those bands I have no idea. Maybe we were lucky or maybe the Lord watched over our hapless little gang.

Bull Rings

Billy Verzuh stopped off one day at the gang's big four-foot marble bull ring on Maroon Avenue, showed us his slingshot, and said, "I can hit a marble in the ring with this." We laughed. No way he could do that.

Billy was older than us, maybe sixteen, and a lot bigger. He had a homemade slingshot, a forked willow branch with an inner tube band, and a pouch for holding the ammo. I had a slingshot I made—hell, we all had them, and there was nothing special looking about Billy's. We took the bait, told him "no way you can hit a marble," and let him have at it.

Well, he pulled a "steelie" marble out of his pocket, put it in the pouch, and reared back. Whack! One glass marble exploded. We were big-eyed, but chalked it up to luck, and challenged him to do it again. Whack! And again. Whack. Marbles shattered. Over and over. He was destroying our marbles! We began to panic, and begged him to quit.

We bought our marbles at the CF&I Company Store using money we had to cajole from our parents, and they were all being ruined! Billy stopped after we whined enough, and afterward, in our eyes, he'd earned swagger rights. It was a truly remarkable feat when you think about it, to be that accurate with a home-made slingshot from standing outside the bull ring.

Playing bull ring marbles was a favorite of the Spaghetti Gang, like the kids in this picture. Library of Congress, Arizona. 1940s.

The bull ring on Maroon Avenue wasn't the only one in town, not by any means. Whenever and wherever we were, if we didn't have much going on we'd take a stick and draw a bull ring in the dirt. The roads weren't paved, and there were very few cars in Crested Butte, so playing in the street was safe enough. We carried our marbles with us at all times so we were always ready for a game.

If you've never played marbles, you might not know how competitive a game it is. Each player puts five marbles in the center of the ring. Using your favorite "shooter" marble, the goal is to knock the other guys' marbles out of the ring. The ones you knock out, you get to keep. If you don't aim right or give it enough power and your shooter stops inside the ring it's at risk of being knocked out (and kept!) by the other players. You could lose your favorite shooter that way, and oh, was it ever hard to win it back.

The miners often stopped to play with us on the way home from their shifts. One time Jiggy Vernon and a few of us were playing when a miner I admired stopped to play. Amadeo Giardino was mellow and soft spoken, a beautiful big-proportioned man who lived with his brother on White Rock. When he stopped to join us in our game, I was amazed. Here we were, little kids, and this big old miner honored us by kneeling in the dirt to play marbles. It was a thrill.

Looking at Amadeo, you'd think a big guy like that wouldn't be scared of anything. I guess he was human, like the rest of us, though, because one dark night a few days after he played marbles with us, he ran over to my folks' house claiming somebody was pounding on his bedroom window trying to get in. Amadeo needed help!

My tough, old, Italian grandma lived with us at the time and was the only adult at home that night. She didn't hesitate. Though she only weighed 110 pounds soaking wet, she'd faced far greater dangers in her life and was brave to the core. She grabbed a pick handle for a weapon, marched ahead of Amadeo, and conquered the source of the pounding—a tree branch banging on the window in the gusts of wind. I didn't admire Amadeo any less after that, but my respect for Grandma sure got elevated a notch or two.

Talk About Heaven

Besides begging for marbles, one other thing we pestered our folks for was enough money to go down to the Company Store to get a treat. There wasn't a lot of spare change lying around back in those days. Everybody worked hard, and everybody was poor, but once in a while we'd scrape together enough money for an ice cream. Then a few of us would head straight to the Company Store, which at the time seemed like a huge place to me, with clothes, groceries, shoes, you name it. A true general store. At the back of the store was an ice cream counter. We'd march back there and the lady knew us from times before and she'd start fixing banana splits, our favorite, the

The banana splits we ate at the CF&I Company Store were heavenly. Courtesy of the Malensek family.

minute she saw us. Those banana splits were six or eight inches long and served in a special shallow oval bowl made just for that purpose. One banana, sliced on the bottom, three kinds of ice cream, chocolate syrup, cherries, coconut, nuts, and caramel syrup, heaped into that bowl. She'd add anything we wanted. Seems like we even had marshmallow cream on 'em. We ate our banana splits slow and deliberate, savoring the treat as long as we could. Talk about heaven!

Smoking Snipes

When we got a little older, the Spaghetti Gang gave up hoops and cops-and-robbers and took up another, less wholesome activity. Our new pastime involved occasionally walking in front of Mattivi's Bar, where the miners sometimes threw their cigarette butts to the ground before they went inside. We'd watch a miner pitch his cigarette butt down into the dirt, then one of us would run over and pick up the butt, which we called a snipe, and put it in a Prince Albert brand tobacco can. The whole time we'd be looking around to make sure nobody saw us.

After we gathered a few snipes we'd head down to our hideaway, which was in some willows below the train depot. We'd pull out the snipes, unwrap the tobacco from the paper, and save the tobacco in another can. Someone always had some cigarette paper and we'd try to roll our own cigarettes from the tobacco we'd collected. Most ended up looking like worms, but it didn't matter. We'd sit back, smoke, and feel like tough guys, at least until we started coughing. I don't know as we liked smoking, but it was something we weren't supposed to do, so it was natural for a bunch of kids to want to try it.

The smoking fell by the wayside for me after my mom discovered bits of tobacco in the front pocket of my bib overalls. Along with receiving a wrath of angry words, I really got whipped. No more smoking for me! I never even retrieved my Prince Albert can, which I'd hidden in a rafter in the outhouse.

After getting caught with smokes, I stuck to the more wholesome Spaghetti Gang activities, like playing marbles. One time on the way to the big bull ring, me and my buddies walked up the street by the hardware store (which I guess was the center of my universe) and some older boys were hosing water into what looked like a balloon. Those balloons kept on getting bigger and bigger till it seemed like they'd never pop. It was shocking how large they got before they burst. I didn't know where those guys had gotten such terrific balloons, and I didn't ask until later on. "Those were Johnny rubbers," I was told, but I still didn't understand until my buddies explained their real purpose—and that's the first I ever heard of condoms. Another piece of my sex education fell into place.

Most of the men in town smoked. A couple of my uncle George Sneller's buddies. Crested Butte, late 1920s.

Sex ed wasn't offered in school back then, so we learned in bits and pieces. Another fragment of my instruction occurred a few days later when one of my Spaghetti Gang buddies stole a small book from his older brother. We scurried down to the hideaway to take a look. It was one of those flip books with stick figures. We took turns fanning the pages and seeing a man and a woman having sex. This was an eye opener, to see this in action.

Hanging with the Spaghetti Gang taught me a lot of things, I suppose, though mostly we just had good clean fun as boys do.

Knife Sticking

Everyone carried a knife up in Crested Butte, no matter their age. It was a normal thing for little kids to carry around four-inch blades. Not that they were good knives, mind you, not by any means, but we had a knife on us at all times—in school, in church, you name it, it didn't matter. I didn't have special church clothes so if the knife was in my pocket, into church it would go.

Crested Butte kids hanging around on Elk Avenue, as they have for generations. Joe Saya is behind the boys. 1920s.

The knives made us feel like real men, but that wasn't their only purpose. We used them for cutting willows and sticks for fires at the hideout, making fishing poles, gutting fish, trimming our fingernails, and whenever else they came in handy. But when we were just hanging around someplace we'd have us a Knife Sticking contest. The goal was to flip your knife from a certain position and have it land point down in the dirt and stick, handle up in the air.

Starting from the hip position, we'd each flip our knife. Whoever's knife stuck without falling over would make the next round, from shoulder position. Each round the winners would graduate up the body, flipping from nose height, ear height, one shoulder, then the other shoulder. Usually by that time everybody was disgusted and tired of the knife game because most of the time the hard dirt in the street was bad for sticking. I don't know if anybody ever made it to the other shoulder. I never practiced much so the game lost its entertainment value early on for me.

Skating on Peanut Lake, early 1900s. Courtesy of the Crested Butte Mountain Heritage Museum, Russ Lallier Collection.

Make-Do Hockey

By the first of November, the streets were too frozen for the knife sticking game, and the long Crested Butte winter had begun. The gang was somewhat curtailed by the cold, though we often managed to play hockey on a pretty good-sized pond past the train depot. Tony Verzuh owned the land and he didn't mind us going down there. We'd bring a bunch of shovels from home and clear off enough snow for a decent sized rink. With hockey sticks we made of thick willows and a make-do puck that was a chunk of coal or some damn thing, we managed to play our version of hockey there. Nobody had skates that really fit. We had to use whatever skates we could borrow.

My ankles were so weak that I skated more or less with my ankles turned in, folding the skates over so bad the leather scraped on the ice and pretty soon the leather would be wore out. I didn't pay much attention to how my feet were feeling because I wanted to play so bad. At the end my poor feet would be numb and blistered, but I couldn't care less. I was part of the gang and the fun. –/–

Chapter 8

Christy and the Cousins

Of all my cousins, I spent the most time with Anton "Christy" Christoff. He was the best man at Phyllis' and my wedding in 1951. Audrey Spann, Phyllis Spann Guerrieri, Richard Guerrieri, "Christy." Married at the Spann Ranch, Gunnison.

New Boots

One of the few things I ever got that was brand new, and I remember precisely, was a lace-up pair of boots with a knife scabbard on the side. My cousin Anton "Christy" Christoff and I had the same kind of boots. We entertained ourselves by having a race to see who could lace the boots fastest using just one hand. A trivial game, but exciting for us. Kids can entertain themselves with a little of nothing, that I know.

Other than those new shoes, I only remember wearing hand-me-downs my whole childhood. There were a helluva lot of kids in town and all the moms traded clothes around. If your pants got a little short-legged, somebody'd notice and before you knew it, your mom would hand you a castoff pair of overalls from somebody or the other, and off you'd go. It was like an underground telegraph system, neighbor to neighbor, mom to mom, sharing the news of who-needs-what.

Most of the time I'd get holes in the soles of my shoes before I outgrew them. Mom taught me how to cut out new cardboard liners in the shape of the sole and that way I'd get by a few more weeks, maybe even make 'em last until winter when I'd wear my galoshes over the top.

Mom patched holes in socks, overalls, and shirts. No one patches things up anymore like they did then. Repairing clothes was a necessity because we couldn't afford new ones, so that's what we did, and so did everyone else. There's no shame in wearing patched clothes when everyone around you is poor and wearing them, too. We looked, dressed, and ate like the people around us, simple as that. I never felt embarrassed about it. Nobody dressed fancy except for special church occasions, which were the only times I remember wearing a pair of pants with a belt (probably borrowed). Otherwise it was overalls, every day of my childhood.

Strap-On Skis

My cousin Christy and I would meet behind the Malensek house at the end of Maroon Avenue where there was a steep hill we could ski on. I'd start from my house, fasten on my skis with bindings consisting of one strap with an inner tube band around the toe. The heel would twist back and forth on the skis, which made skiing tricky. I don't remember if we used ski poles or not. I skied past the second Coal Creek Bridge, up the street past the old Catholic Church to where Christy waited for me.

We'd stair-step up that steep hill, and if we were lucky it was packed firm and we could herringbone up, which was much faster. After we struggled our way up the hill we'd come whipping down that hill with plenty of speed, flying down Maroon Avenue as far as we could go. Then back up again, and another adrenaline rush on the way down. We wore out quick enough without a ski lift to take us to the top, but oh, the fun we had on the way down.

We wore out quick enough without a ski lift. Crested Butte, 1930s or 1940s.

One day Christy and I took off on skis toward the old Peanut Mine. From there we tromped up the hill through the quakie trees. We stopped, packed down a spot, and prepared to cook our food. Christy had a little stove kit with a small metal tripod stand and a metal plate on it. There were these small white pills, quarter size, that you set on the underneath plate. We struck a match to the pill, which made a very hot flame and heated our water and cooked our food. It was fancy camping equipment for the times.

What a beautiful thing for a kid to sit back and relax after eating. After a time, we skied through the deep snow and back to town. We thought we were in hog heaven with our fancy cook stove and independence on our big excursion.

Ptarmigans

A few weeks later, Christy and I took off again on our skis, going cross-country up beyond town toward Peanut Lake. There was a lot of open ground out there at the time, a swampy area with small ponds and willows.

Christy and I were gliding in that direction when we came upon a flock of beautiful white birds huddled together on the snow in that swamp area. There were so many birds it was like looking at a sea of white feathers. They blended into the snow so

Christy and I would sometimes take off together on our skis. I've never forgotten those adventures. Crested Butte, 1940s.

well that we were nearly upon them before we saw them. We stopped and stared at them for a long time.

Hundreds of those small white birds, about the size of a grouse, just sitting there. They were so beautiful, neither of us made a sound. We just turned away, careful not to spook them, and they stayed right where they were.

Decades later, I found out they were ptarmigans. Ptarmigans turn white in winter and have been seen in high mountain towns in Colorado, but it was the only time I ever saw ptarmigans in Crested Butte. We were mesmerized by the sight of them, which made such an impression on me I never forgot.

I didn't know why so many of those birds were there that day, and why Christy and I were fortunate enough to come across them. Sometimes you look for meaning in such things but never do figure it out.

Someone Watching Over Me

Christy and I liked to go up behind his house and make a very large mound of snow, pack it, and let it set for a few days. He and his family lived in a company owned house on what they now call The Bench but at the time we called it Big Mine Hill.

There was plenty of snow up there for our purposes, and once our mound was pretty well settled, we'd dig the snow out of the center and have ourselves an igloo big enough for both of us to go inside. We'd squeeze through the small opening we called a door and sit around until we eventually got cold. By no means was it warm in there, but for a while it wasn't really cold either. The sunlight came through the snow, so it was surprisingly light inside.

Aunt Donna and Uncle Tony Christoff, Christy's parents. I don't know why the hell they're holding that bird. They lived in company housing up on Big Mine Hill, where I spent a lot of time. Nobody paid much attention back then to what kids were doing, so someone else must've been watching over me. Crested Butte, 1940s.

We thought we were pretty cool to be able to build an igloo. Nobody paid much attention to what we were doing or took notice, and I suppose if one of our igloos had caved in it would have smothered us. Just one more example of why I think someone has been watching over me.

Funny—In Retrospect

Christy wasn't my only cousin by any means. My grandma and grandpa had fourteen kids and as a result I was one of twenty-five grandkids, all of us first cousins—and that was just on the Guerrieri side of the family. Naturally, some cousins in my age group hung around with the Spaghetti Gang, and like I say, we were good kids for the most part. My cousin Gaspar (we called him Gap), however, got a little too rambunctious the time he got a new Red Rider BB Gun.

Gap was up in his bedroom on the second floor of their house on White Rock when down in the street came old man Verzuh's grocery delivery horse and cart

For all I know my cousin Gap's BB gun is still sealed in the rafters at 430 White Rock Avenue. Courtesy of Gunnison County property records, 2017.

plodding along. Gap, wanting to test the accuracy of his new BB gun in the worst way, took careful aim out the window and "Pop!" the Red Rider hit its mark—the big rump of that quiet horse. Quiet no more! The horse went tearing off down the street, groceries flying. Tony Verzuh went to cursing and trying to stop that spooked gelding. Gap's dad, my uncle Jim, happened to be home doing a little work on the house and once he saw that bolting horse it didn't take him a minute to figure out what happened. He came a-roaring up the stairs to Gap's room and snatched the Red Rider.

Mrs. Mattivi met the trick-or-treaters at the door with a fire hose and let 'em have it.

He gave Gap hell, to be sure, but at the same time he didn't want Verzuh to find out who shot his horse and make the family pay for all them groceries. Uncle Jim took that Red Rider and nailed it behind some roofing boards upstairs, and there it stayed, which made Gap miserable for a good long time. For all I know the Red Rider could still be in the rafters of that house on White Rock Avenue.

Gap was a bit of an ornery kid and folks around town knew it. That year when he went trick-or-treating with the Spaghetti Gang, old Mrs. Mattivi didn't greet them too fondly. Mrs. Mattivi met the trick-or-treaters at the door with a fire hose and let 'em have it. Then she called the cops on the drenched trick-or-treaters. Darned if a deputy sheriff didn't show up and the scared gang ran home, candy or no candy. Decades later, the escapades of my cousin Gap are funny, but at the time, I tried to stay clear of his more rowdy adventures.

A Baseball Upside the Head

The town of Crested Butte fielded a decent baseball team and played the nearby towns of Jacks Cabin, Almont, and Gunnison. Although I was never a baseball player, some of my cousins were on the team, so I, along with everyone else in town, went to see the local boys play during the summer.

As I recall, at least four of the Carricato boys, our neighbors, were on the team. There were eight Carricato brothers and that family could have fielded the whole damn team. They were good players from a good family. A left-handed hitter named John Krizmanich was a good player, too.

The Crested Butte women's softball team 1937. The only women I recognize are my cousin Rose Guerrieri Carricato, standing on the upper left, and my aunt Kathryn Sneller Guerrieri, next to her.

John Krizmanich, a left hander, hit the foul ball that knocked me cold. The Crested Butte Baseball Team in the 1940s. Kneeling (left to right), Murph Mufich (coach), Murph Mufich Jr., Art Welch, Ernie Carricato, Frank Carricato. Standing (left to right), Mark Byouk, Leonard Kapushion, Jake Kochevar, John Krizmanich, Pete Spritzer, Joe Savoren, Whitey Sporcich, Chick Mufich, Frank Bruno, Otto Carricato.

One time I was sitting too close to the foul line when Krizmanich smacked the ball foul. Before I could move, that ball smacked me upside of the head and down I went. For a few moments, things went black and someone fetched old Doctor Alford. When I came to, I had a lump—a helluva lump. Doc Alford took a look at me and told my folks I was lucky to be alive. If I'd been hit an inch one way or another, the ball would have killed me. Once again, someone was either watching over me or I'm just hard headed. –/–

Chapter 9

Culture and Me– My Folks Really Tried

No one looks too happy about their First Communion. St. Patrick's Church on Maroon Avenue. Gibson Ridge in the background. Crested Butte, 1926.

I was always fidgeting, thinking about playing marbles, going swimming, or fishing. Somehow I made it through catechism and received my First Communion. Me, on the left, and my aunt Donna Christoff, middle. Crested Butte, 1938.

The Dreaded Catechism

EACH SUMMER THE CATHOLIC CHURCH SENT NUNS TO teach us catechism to prepare us for our first communions. Catechism took place at the schoolhouse and my folks signed me up. I had a hard time concentrating because it was summer days outside and I could have been doing a lot of fun things besides sitting there listening to them nuns. I was always fidgeting, thinking about playing marbles, going swimming, or fishing. Catechism seemed to go on forever, but probably lasted two or three weeks, which would have been fine if it was only for one summer. But you didn't just graduate and get your catechism in one year. No. Those nuns would come every year. Every year another catechism school. Oh, how I dreaded it.

Lucille, me, and Pauline around 1944, all dressed up for some darn church thing or another. Crested Butte.

Somehow, I made it through and received my communion. Some part of what the nuns drilled into me must've stuck because I got so I rather liked attending masses and would even go to prayer sessions during the week.

My cousin Eva Christoff sang in the church choir. The choir was located in the balcony above the congregation and I would go up there sometimes and try to pretend I was part of the choir. I'd mouth the words with no sound coming out, not to be ornery but because I loved everything about church and wanted to sit up there.

I was such a regular that the priest eventually invited me over to his house. He always served me cookies. After I went over a couple times, he asked me to commit to even more religion and become a priest later in life. That was it for me. I didn't like the idea of being pressured to become a priest. I never went to his house again, and religion faded.

Flying Dots on the Page

My folks were bound and determined to give me the enrichments they lacked in their own childhoods. One summer they started me on piano lessons with Helen Morgan. She lived catty-corner across Maroon Avenue from us with her husband, Tim.

I was supposed to go over to her house and practice two or three times a week. Too many times I'd be on the street playing marbles or something and forget about my piano lesson and my practices. My mom would inevitably find out and I'd get a whipping.

She was a good teacher, Mrs. Morgan, and even with all my forgetting I managed to learn enough that she thought I should participate in the damn recital, which was held over at the high school. I was supposed to wear a tie and on the day of the recital, I fought with my tie for some time trying to tie it properly. No one was home to help me, so I walked across the street to ask Old Man Lunk if he could tie it for me. Lunk was a German fellow, not very tall, but sturdy built. He and his wife had a daughter quite a lot older than me who was quite pretty, and a son by the name of Rudy who was my friend.

The old man agreed to tie it for me, and afterwards I said, "Thank you very much," because I was quite appreciative.

He looked me right in the eye, and with a straight face said, "I'll tell you one thing," his voice serious as hell, "I can't buy anything with a thank you."

I ended up taking lessons long enough so I could play what I thought was pretty well, but I never liked it.

My folks tried to steer me toward refined skills, but the cowboy life attracted me early on. Me, with my cousin Marie Guerrieri, left. Crested Butte 1937.

I was dumbfounded and didn't quite comprehend. He wasn't making a joke, and I wondered if he expected me to pay him something. I said thanks one more time, left his house, and headed for the dreaded recital, but I never understood Lunk's attitude and I never forgot it.

I got to the recital, tie in place, and there were the parents, grandparents, aunts and uncles, all cleaned up, and looking up at the stage where the piano was placed, waiting for their little Johnny or Jenny to play, all the moms and dads thinking their kid would someday be a great piano player. Half the audience seemed like they were my relatives, and pretty soon it came my turn. I walked up the steps to the stage and made the mistake of looking at the crowd, which made me even more shook up than I already was, seeing that whole batch of people staring at me. It didn't matter how much I had practiced (which probably wasn't enough), I was nervous as hell when I got to the piano. I looked at the music and it was as if I'd never seen music notes in my life, with all the flying dots on the sheet. Lo and behold, I somehow got through my piece but I messed up on plenty of notes.

I ended up taking lessons long enough so I could play what I thought was pretty well, but I never liked it. I cried and fought with my folks, begging them to let me quit. Eventually they agreed, thinking I was hopeless, I'm sure.

Dot Dot Dash

After that, my folks got the idea that learning Morse code would be of benefit to me. The telegraph operator down at the railroad station agreed to teach me. He was one of them old guys with a cap with a green visor, just like you see in the old photos. I can't remember his name but he was a nice fellow and I attended his lessons numerous times at the old depot. He tried to teach me the alphabet, sending me home with a piece of paper so I could practice. Over and over he would tell me dot dot means this, dot dash means that, but who wants to work on that kinda stuff when you could slink outside and go fishing. Morse code went by the wayside just like the piano. –/–

One summer my folks engaged the telegraph operator at the Crested Butte Train Depot, who tried to teach me Morse code. Courtesy of the Crested Butte Mountain Heritage Museum.

Chapter 10

Summer Jobs, Because Darn Near Anything's Better than Catechism

The Niccoli bunkhouse, where I stayed when I made my debut as a sheepherder. Crested Butte, 2016.

Milk Delivery Boys

Once I got rid of piano lessons and Morse code, I had the opportunity to do what I'd always wanted to do, which was to help Bill Lacy deliver milk around town. Bill was about my age and was my buddy. His son owns Lacy Construction in Crested Butte.

Bill's folks had a ranch way down on East River with some dairy cows they milked. They brought the milk to town and bottled it and that summer Bill and I would put the bottles in a wagon with one of us pulling the handle and the other keeping his hand on the wagon to keep it from turning over as we went over all those clumps in the streets. We'd stop at every household signed up to buy milk and deliver those quart jars of milk. We'd put them on the porch and pick up the empties left out for us.

I was quite comfortable sitting on the wagon or sled waiting for Martin, knowing the weight would stop the horse if need be.

Lacy owned a real gentle big dog that followed us around as we made our deliveries. One day we got the bright idea to make that dog pull the wagon. We spent the better part of a day building a harness for that dog, although how we managed to find enough ropes and straps for it, I don't know. The harness worked pretty good and the dog managed to pull the wagon for us. We were damn careful, worried the whole time that the dog might run away and break all those milk bottles. If that happened, what were the people gonna do? I hate to think of the kind of trouble we would have been in. Now that I think back on it, the way that dog plodded along, there weren't no way he was gonna run away. Most likely he was so old he was half dead.

After I got my start delivering with Bill, I talked my way into helping with grocery delivery for George Spehar's store(shown in the photo on page 72). The Spehar's hired hand, a fellow by the name of Martin, drove a one-horse hitch to bring the groceries around town. He was a real nice man who would let me drive the horse but he'd keep his hands on the reins behind mine. At each house, he'd stop and take out a weight, a steel block that must have weighed 60 pounds, which he'd set on the ground. The weight was attached to the bridle in such a way that if the horse moved, the weight would stop him. I was quite comfortable sitting on the wagon or sled waiting for Martin, knowing the weight would stop the horse if need be. It was an exciting time in a small way to drive that horse.

Of course, I didn't get paid for these 'jobs,' but I was busy, happy, and out of my ma's hair.

An Aggravating Breed of Animal

The following summer I managed to work for Frank Niccoli herding his sheep, which he kept over at Sid Niccoli's place on the west side of Slate River, across from what is now Crested Butte South. Frank had about twenty or thirty head of sheep, and these weren't the kind of nice, pretty sheep you see nowadays with the pretty wool on them. The wool on Frank's sheep didn't look much good and none of the sheep matched each other. Some of Frank's sheep were black-faced, some white-faced, and I think he got them cheap because they were renegades.

I stayed in a nice log cabin 50 yards from Sid's main house. Sid would get me up each morning and I'd wash my face in the ditch running between the road and the main house. The water was colder than hell and I'd wake up with a jolt. After I washed up I'd go in for breakfast. Sid's wife, Justina, was a good cook and always had something ready for me to eat. She brought the food out to the porch, and also gave me a lunch to take with me.

After breakfast, Sid helped me saddle the broken-down, gentle horse they had me ride. Then he'd help me drive the sheep, which we kept in the corral each night, across Highway 135 and over the railroad track to the hilly sage pasture where they grazed. My job was to stay all day with the sheep, keep them in the right meadow, and bring them back to the corral in the evening. Because the fences were built for cattle, it was easy for sheep to go through if someone didn't turn them away.

The sheep-grazing land ran south from where Bob Niccoli's house sits now to the stock lane and north to what is now the Spann ranches. I was to keep the sheep within those boundaries.

The job was less difficult than it was boring and monotonous. For a kid to sit there, all by myself, for hours and hours, got tiresome. Lucky for me the sheep kept me somewhat busy. I'd get them to where I thought they were settled in for grazing, then I'd get off the old horse to relax. Nine times out of ten, as soon as I sat down, those damn sheep would be on the move and at the other fence line in nothing flat. I'd scramble to get back on the old horse, positioning him on the hill so it was easier to get back on and then take off after the sheep to get ahead of them. The whole day was like that, on and off, on and off that old horse all day long. Up and down and around the pasture I'd go, trying to keep those sheep contained.

I never knew what happened to the sheep, whether they sheared them for the wool or butchered them for the meat. After my herding job, sheep didn't interest me enough to ask.

GEORGE
GENERAL

After a summer working with Sid Niccoli's sheep, I didn't want anything more to do with that breed of animal. A flock of sheep belonging to the Pecharich family coming down Elk Avenue in 1943. Courtesy of the Crested Butte Mountain Heritage Museum & Pecharich family in loving memory of Josephine Pecharich.

I must've got paid a little for that job because that would have been my only incentive for sticking with it. The job and the sheep were uninspiring, so that was the first and last time I agreed to be around sheep. I never wanted anything more to do with that breed of animal.

A Horse Named SOB

In the summer after sixth grade, I got a haying season job from Chuck Halazon. He owned the ranch where the Crested Butte Community School is now.

Back in the day when ranchers hayed with horses and loose haystacks were the only option, somebody had the unglamorous job of supervising the stacker horse. In the summer of 1943 on the Halazon ranch, that somebody was me. Chuck owned a Jenkins style stacker. You can still see it, standing off Highway 135 near the school. It worked somewhat like a front-end loader. Guys driving the horse-drawn doodlebug rakes and buckrakes filled the bucket of the stacker with loose hay. Then the stacker horse went to work, heaving against the pulleys that elevated the hay up and onto the stack.

There was an art to creating those beautiful loose haystacks. A stacker horse and a team with the bullrake at the Malensek ranch in the 1930s, which was at the base of what is now the Crested Butte ski area. Courtesy of the Malensek family.

As the fellow in charge of the stacker horse, I spent a lot of time waiting around. Waiting for the rakes to come with more hay and waiting for Chuck to call down to me from the top of the stack when he was ready for me to send up another load of hay. After setting the stacker gauges the way Chuck wanted 'em for each load, I'd head over to make the stubborn stacker horse pull. I wasn't a very big kid, always skinny, and I would tug and heave with all my 100 pounds on that horse. Sometimes, I'd get him going, and just when I was feeling pleased and the hay was way up in the air that darn horse would balk, stopping dead in his tracks. There I'd be, with the hay halfway up in the air, and me pulling and pulling and the horse not moving.

Old Chuck Halazon's stacker still stands next to Highway 135 in Crested Butte. The Crested Butte Community School is in the background. 2016.

Chuck would come down off the stack, running over to where I was and he'd start poking the horse's ribs and hollering a certain word with the initials SOB, which is the only name I ever heard him call that horse. Every time he poked, he'd holler that word. When this was happening, I was running frantically to stay ahead, so that if the horse called SOB took off, I could stop him before the pulleys were torn out of the stacker.

Later on, if SOB balked again and Chuck saw what was happening, he'd start to hollering from above, "You goddamn SOB." If I was lucky Chuck's bellowing would be enough and away we'd go, me leading, SOB pulling, hay moving! Other times, Chuck would have to come down off the stack, and after plenty of cussing and some poking, we'd have success for several more loads.

Chuck never offered to pay me for my work, and I never asked to be paid. I wanted to be outside and around horses anytime I could.

Pack a Goddamn Lunch

One summer Christy and I got hired to go around the fence at Sid Niccoli's. Our job was to check for broken wires and patch any we found. Sid told us we didn't need to pack a lunch. It wasn't a big job, and he'd pick us up around noon.

Well, we finished going around the fence and waited back where Sid had dropped us off that morning, at the old house on his upper place. Noon came and went. No ride. We got hungrier and hungrier until we thought we were downright starving.

A big patch of rhubarb behind the house caught our eye and as we sat there getting more and more famished, that sour rhubarb looked tastier and tastier. We got to eating those stalks of rhubarb and boy did they hit the spot. We didn't feel so famished as long as we were chewing on rhubarb. By the time Sid finally showed up in late afternoon, we'd eaten a good amount of rhubarb.

You might think our guts would rebel from that tart rhubarb, but we felt just fine, and it wasn't until the next morning that both of us broke out in a red rash head to toe. Our folks were ready to call Doc Alford again until we told them about the rhubarb. Who knows what he would've diagnosed and prescribed, especially if he'd been drinking that day.

My cousin Ernest "Swede" Guerrieri and I had a damn poor lunch that day in the 1940s, years before this photo of him was taken.

The spots went away over the course of a few hours, but my aversion to raw rhubarb stuck with me the rest of my life. I love rhubarb baked in a pie, but I've never eaten another fresh stalk.

Some years later in the early spring it was my job, along with my cousin Ernest Guerrieri (who we always called "Swede" but I don't know why) to go fix the fence up in Lost Canyon for my uncle Pasquale "Charlie" Guerrieri. I guess I hadn't learned my lesson about bringing a lunch the first time because it was the same story. We were supposed to be done by noon, no need to pack a lunch, Uncle was going to pick us up.

Well, we finished the fence and headed back toward the meeting spot but it was a long walk to our ride. We walked and walked until we got so hungry our bellies felt like they were touching our backbones. After ambling down through some quakies, we ran across a dead doe, semi-frozen. I don't know if we did too much thinking or deciding whether it was the right thing to do or not, but it only took us a few minutes to skin enough of the doe to get some nice back straps. We built a fire and had a hell of a time getting those straps cooked because the meat was partially frozen and all we had to cook it on were some sharpened sticks. We'd burn the outside a bit but it'd still be too raw in the middle to eat. After a time, we got the outside done enough to eat and managed to scrape off a couple chunks, one for each of us. Between bites, Swede and I agreed it was the best meat we ever tasted, though neither of us could stomach a second piece.

We tamped down the fire and got to the meeting place on time, but it was a familiar story—no ride. We had to wait another two hours before Uncle Charlie came to pick us up. Good thing we ate that "delicious" meat.

Decades afterwards, I still pack a little food darn near wherever I go. –/–

Chapter 11

Into the Mine

When I rode into the mine on top of a coal car similar to this one, Dad showed me how to push myself off and away from the car in case the mule lost control on the down grades. CF&I Colorado mine, courtesy of the Steelworks Center.

My folks gave me a brand-new bike, an unbelievable gift. With my sisters, Pauline and Lucille, around 1941. Crested Butte.

Free as a Breeze

WE WERE STILL LIVING IN THE HOUSE BEHIND THE HARDWARE STORE when my folks bought me a brand-new bicycle. An unbelievable gift, shiny and black, and a real beauty—at least while it was new.

Once I got that bike I was free to take off fishing wherever I pleased. I'd dig some worms at home and put them in a Prince Albert tobacco can, collect my homemade willow fishing pole and peddle to the Slate River Bridge. I almost always caught fish, not so much from the big stream, but from a warm-water spring entering the Slate just before the bridge. I caught plenty of trout in that hole there. It was quite a bicycle trip, but oh, didn't it feel good to take some fish home for supper.

I felt free as a breeze riding my bike and sometimes I'd even ride to the Bulkley Mine loading area, a couple miles out of town. There was a mine caretaker living in a small house next to the tracks there. I'd stop at the house and his wife always gave me something to eat. She was a very mellow lady with somewhat of a deformed hand. I'd spend hours outside with her, cutting off dandelion heads and making chains out of the stems.

She also had a big ole tank with goldfish of every size and color you could imagine. She loved them and I had fun watching them because I hadn't seen that kind of fish before. What the hell she did with them in the winter, I have no idea, because that tank woulda froze solid.

The Gravity of His Work

There was no way my bike would make it up the steep zigzag trail to the mine to see my dad at work, so I rode as far as I could, then walked the rest of the way. I liked to visit him where he worked, outside the shaft. He had a very intense job of sending those heavy loaded coal carts down the hill on the tram from the mine to land just right at the tipple.

The tipple was the place where the loaded coal cars coming out of the mine were "tipped" into the waiting train cars.

My dad, Geniali "Gene" Guerrieri, once took me into the tunnels of the Bulkley Mine. Gunnison, 1980s.

Concentration was the key to Dad's job because any mistake on his part would result in a major disaster, stoppage, and lost productivity. One time, the guy who had the job before him didn't get the cars stopped and they went plowing through and off the tipple. Talk about a mess.

I'd show up to watch and Dad would be behind a six or eight foot diameter brake drum which had a cable thick as my wrist running 'round it. Next to the drum were tracks where the empty coal cars stopped on top, and beside them, another set of tracks for lowering full coal cars. A shed roof over the tipple track kept the snow off of the tracks.

The grade of the tramway was so steep the drum operator couldn't see the cars at the bottom as he lowered them. Fifty yards from where he stood, the cars disappeared over a hump in the hill. He only knew how low the cars were by marks on the cable. When a certain mark reached the drum, he'd know to put the breaks on so the coal cars would land safely at the tipple.

Dad's job was repetitious. Empty cars up, full cars down. Over and over. As soon as the empties came up he would first set the brake using a big handle he pulled. A simple pull wouldn't do the trick to stop the heavy coal cars. Dad used the weight of his whole body to stop the brake drum. He even fashioned a stirrup attached to the handle to give him more leverage.

After Dad set the brake he'd grab the sprag, which was a three or four-foot piece of wood tapered at both ends, and jam it between the spokes of the brake wheel and the frame so the wheel couldn't move.

He was always on the lookout to see if the drum cable was starting to wear. Just as disastrous as a brake operator losing the cars down the tipple would be a sudden break in the cable. When Dad saw a worn spot, he'd stop to splice the cable. I watched him splice one time, and it wasn't an easy thing to do. First, he separated the metal strands of cable using sharp tapered steel spikes. Then he wove the spliced piece into the strands one by one, using his fingers and the spikes. Each splice was four or five feet long and had to be tapered just right in order to run smoothly through the drum. It took a lot of finger strength to make a good splice. An impressive skill. Dad was careful and smart and never lost a load.

Watching him at work was fascinating enough to keep a fidgety kid like me, who these days would likely be put on medication to slow me down, quiet and still. I must've understood the gravity of his work because I never got in the way or bothered

The huge hand-operated brake drum Dad operated. Charles "Chuckie" Guerrieri hiked up to the old Bulkley mine and took this picture in the 1980s, decades after the mine had closed.

My cousins Fortes and Gus Veltri in front of the CF&I tipple in the early 1930s. Fortes had crutches because he was born with spina bifida. He ended up living an interesting and fulfilling life as a musician. Crested Butte.

him. If I was told to sit, I sat. If I was told to be quiet, I was quiet.

There were times when there was no waiting train, so there were no cars to send down the tipple. That's when Dad tended to the other part of his job, shoeing the Bulkley Mine mules. The Bulkley used a good number of mules, not as many as the Big Mine, of course, but mules were important to any mining operation for pulling the cars in and out of the shafts.

Mules are cantankerous, and farrier work is a backbreaking task, so shoeing them was not an easy thing to do. There was a forge right there opposite the brake drum, and Dad somehow learned enough about iron-work that he was able to shape the shoes for mules. Always a kind man who cared about animals, Dad made sure the mules' feet were well shod.

Dad had backbone and wasn't afraid to take on any task if he thought he could make a buck, and it's always amazed me that he succeeded at most everything he tried. Coal-mining, mule-shoeing, ranching, you name it. He did it all. How that wiry man done all them things in his life I'll never know.

An Eerie Trip

Even though he didn't work inside the mine, on occasion Dad had to take a cart in or out of a shaft. One day when I was visiting him at work, he took me inside the Bulkley on the coal cars. A mule pulled the cars, of course, and the trip involved some steep grades as well as some flat surfaces. I thought riding in a coal car was a pretty swell experience, at least for awhile. As we got further and further in, though, the few lights along the way barely lit up the dark tunnel and the temperature dropped until I was near shivering.

It was an eerie feeling, riding along in that creaky, uncomfortable car, the mule plodding along, with a light only every once in awhile pointing the way.

When we got to a certain shaft running perpendicular to the tracks, Dad stopped the mule. I scrambled off the empty coal car and we walked in. The shaft was well timbered on the sides and on the roof and Dad used his headlamp so we knew where to go.

About twenty or thirty yards into the tunnel, we came upon Uncle Paul and Uncle Charlie. They wore rain gear because tunnel roofs dripped water constantly in the

Crested Butte coal miners, early 1900s.

mines. I didn't have a raincoat and felt my hair and shoulders getting wet. Uncle Paul and Uncle Charlie wore helmets with carbide lamps attached and they were intent on digging coal, their pickax and shovels swinging as they loaded chunks into a waiting coal car. Their faces were black like you see in pictures of miners, with only the whites of their eyes and their teeth visible in the dark. To me they looked like black ghosts. My dad talked to them for a few minutes and then led me back to the main tunnel.

There we swapped the empty coal cars for some loaded ones on the side rail, Dad hitching the mule to the heavy cars for the trip out. The cars were square with about a 45-degree lip on top to keep the coal in. Dad threw a few sprags onto the cars and instructed me to sit on the lip with my feet dangling and to hold on—with two hands. Before we got going he also showed me how to push myself off and away from the car in case something went wrong. In a mine, there's always an element of danger and you've gotta be careful. He sat on the opposite side of the car, facing forward, with his feet on the hitch attached to the mule. Away we went with the mule straining as he pulled and the cars rattling. It was a rough and noisy ride. Any time we approached a down grade, that old mule would start to clenching back on the britchen strap to hold the load and my dad would jump off and use two or three sprags, shoving them in the wheels to help hold the weight. After placing the sprags he'd run and jump back on the car. When we hit level ground, he'd step off and release the sprags.

Young as I was, the hazards of mine work were clear to me. That was the first and the last time I ever went into the mine. I was spooked. I was around junior high age about then.

Imagine a person that young seeing all those men and especially my dad working so hard in such danger. I can still hear and see the big drum whirling and the cars making loud clickety-clack noises. Now, at almost 85 years old, thinking back on it, I feel blessed to have seen first hand the real work of the miners.

Along with his regular job of running the tipple cars and shoeing the mules, for a while Dad also took on a third role at the mine—mule caretaker. The Bulkley Mine mule barn was much smaller than the Big Mine barn, with maybe a dozen mules, but somebody had to feed and harness them and get them ready each day. There was a small house at the mine where the mule caretaker could live, but the place was in a state of disrepair, so all year long, summer, winter, fall, spring, my dad would make the long trek from town and get to the mule barn an hour earlier than everyone else in order to get the mules ready for the day's work.

On the lucky days I was allowed to help Dad with the mules, one of my jobs was to give them their morning grain. There was a huge wooden grain bin in the mule barn, and grain troughs in each stall, along with a runway in front of the stalls where hay bales were stacked. I enjoyed going down the runway, pouring grain into the troughs, and knowing I was helping my dad and the mules.

For drinking water, the mules had a year-round warm-water spring in the mule corrals, which was piped and gravity-fed into a water trough.

In winter, almost all the miners rode the cars because the terrain was treacherous for horses in the snow and the trail prone to snow slides.

The inside of the Bulkley Mine, where a lot of my relatives worked, was dark and wet. 1940s.

After the mules were fed and watered, Dad got them harnessed up. Miners would show up, some riding their horses up the zigzag trail to the top if it was summertime and others hitching a ride in the empty rail cars coming to the top. In winter, almost all the miners rode the cars because the terrain was treacherous for horses in the snow and the trail prone to snow slides.

I can still picture those miners riding the cars toward the waiting mules, and I imagine them talking and joking, always in the backs of their minds thinking how to jump off if something happened—if a cable broke, if a car jumped the tracks, and how they'd get away when all hell broke loose.

The men who rode horses up to the mine left their horses in the mule barn during their shift, and being the mule caretaker, Dad was allowed to keep all of his riding horses there, too, which was handy since we lived in town and didn't have much room for a horse. Dad kept his own horses in separate stalls from the mules and

My dad worked his horses hard every day and he took good care of them so they were in top physical condition. Dad and me in 1942 with his mare Pearl. Crested Butte.

miners' horses, and always gave them whole oats and hay. Their grain bins were always full, which is an unusual and expensive way to keep a horse fed. Too much grain can cause colic for a horse, a bad deal, sometimes fatal, but Dad started a horse out slow with whole grain, cutting back the hay until the horse had oats in front of him all the time. He worked his horses hard, every day, and he needed them to be in top physical condition. Grain kept them fleshy and strong, and this drew the notice of the Bulkley Mine owner, a fellow by the name of Palmgreen.

Whenever Palmgreen came to town to inspect the mine, he always asked to ride one of Dad's horses, the one called Daisy, not only because she was bomb-proof but also well kept, nice looking, and had a shiny coat. Palmgreen wouldn't ride any other horse, which was a source of pride for my dad. –/–

Chapter 12

Stars in the Windows

My sisters Lucille (left) and Pauline (right) with our cousin Jimmy Christoff, around 1944, Crested Butte.

A Pall Around Town

World War II affected everyone in America, even a seemingly carefree kid in a tiny coal mining town in Colorado. Most of the men a few years older than me enlisted, guys I'd known my whole life. The rest of us, both kids and adults, tried to help the war effort in whatever way we could. I remember saving the aluminum foil from gum wrappers, which my mom put into a large ball which we'd drop off at the general store in town to be sent to factories and the like for recycling. Anything the military asked people to save, we'd do our best.

We were poor before the war, but with rationing, times got especially tough. My folks saved up our gas coupons so we'd have enough fuel to drive to the tipple on Sundays in Dad's Model T truck. There we'd walk along the steep tramway and pick up the free chunks of coal that had fallen off the cars.

My sisters and I had the job of gathering the coal and stuffing it into gunnysacks. The incline along the tracks was very steep and we had to kind of crawl along as we filled the sacks. The grade was too steep to stand. Once we got our sacks full my folks would drag them back to the truck, which was not an easy chore, even though it was downhill. After enough Sundays of this, we'd have enough coal to heat our house in winter.

Maybe these days kids would argue and refuse to do that kind of chore, but we didn't grow up that way. It was just the thing we did on Sundays. That was that. I also suppose that somewhere in the back of our minds we knew how cold we'd be the next winter if we didn't do our part.

During the war, when the Spaghetti Gang walked around the streets of Crested Butte, there was a bit of a pall over us as most of the houses in town had cloth stars hung in their windows. Each star represented someone from that house in the service. I think the blue stars indicated "in the service" and the red stars meant "killed in action." Very few houses up there didn't have stars.

Very few houses up there didn't have stars on them.

So many men from town joined up that the mine finally made a formal request for the military to stop enlisting people from Crested Butte because there were barely enough men left to keep the mine running. Of course, the coal coming out of the mine was necessary for the war effort, too.

Albert Lee Manley. Courtesy of Wes Bailey, V.F.W. Post 4665. 1943.

Albert Lee Manley

Out of the men from Crested Butte who were killed in action, the one that hit home for me was Albert Manley. He was the brother of a girl named Loretta, who was in my class. She and I were very good friends. I'll never forget her. She was a rather, how shall I say it, nice looking girl, but she had a kinda bow-legged walk, nothing distracting but a unique stride. She used to come over to visit with my girl cousins Eva and Genevieve Christoff, and that's how I got to know her.

I've attended almost all class reunions to this day and I never saw Loretta Manley again. I've often wondered about Loretta over the years.

A. Wesley Bailey, Jr. Courtesy of Wes Bailey, V.F.W. Post 4665. 1941.

My cousin Jimmy Christoff. Courtesy of Wes Bailey, V.F.W. Post 4665. 1942.

Jimmy Christoff and Wes Bailey

My cousin Jim Christoff enlisted in the Navy and like every family with fellows in the service, we waited anxiously for his letters. When he did write, which wasn't too often, his letters were not very informative. They were censored heavily, with many of the words blacked out, especially anything that might hint at where he was or what his unit was doing.

During those war years, everyone in town kept the radio blaring, hoping for any news from overseas. We scoured the newspapers which showed maps of where the war was being fought, and read the battle articles taking up the front page of every issue, trying to piece together which of our boys' divisions or troops were involved and where.

Those were tough years in our little town, and I still get a little melancholy thinking about the men who went to war.

There were, of course, a few diversions from the war news. Boxing was a very popular sport back then, and whenever Joe Louis had a fight we'd all be glued to the radio to hear the fight announcer. The other radio and newspaper stories that really held our attention were the ones about Man o' War, the thoroughbred racehorse. I think that horse went down in the annals of horse racing history as one of the best. The best part about news of Joe Louis and Man o' War was for small amounts of time we forgot about the war. Then reality would intrude again.

Those were tough years in our little town, and I still get a little melancholy thinking about the men who went to war. I knew most of them. Some were scarred for life from their terrible ordeals. Some, like Wes Bailey, a prisoner of war, went through hell and became an outstanding man after the war.

When Jimmy came back, his complexion was pale and his eyes were bloodshot. For a time, he turned to alcohol, and argued with his dad constantly. It took awhile before he straightened up, but he became a good man and led a decent life.

Several years after Jimmy returned, when I was already married and having kids, I hired him to build a screen fence in the yard to keep our kids safe from the road next to the house. He never talked about his war experiences much, but he was a different person, not the fun-loving young man he was before his time in the service. We still get a Christmas card each year from his daughter in Idaho.

War in the Attic

While Jimmy was away at the war, his brother Christy and I were sometimes allowed to play with Jimmy's train set. It filled almost the whole attic of the Christoff house on Maroon Avenue, with its train tunnels and bridges, miniature houses, hotels, general store, saloon, and the like. Christy and I were careful with the set—it would've been a terrible thing to break Jimmy's train.

The one thing missing in the attic, as far as we were concerned, were airplane bombers, so we went about building them ourselves. We bought some little airplane kits made of balsawood wings and tails and added bombardier equipment. Namely, this consisted of tiny rolled up funnels made of school notebook paper, just large enough to hold a marble bomb. We taped these paper funnels to the planes, along with sewing pins for crosshairs so we could aim our bombs and hit the target with precision.

My God, we got a lot of snow back then. Joe Pecharich delivering coal with his team Prince and Dick. Photo taken on Elk Avenue near the Company Store, 1943. Courtesy of the Crested Butte Mountain Museum & Pecharich family in loving memory of Josephine Pecharich.

We'd fly along, round and round the train set, making airplane noises, and drop the marble at just the right time, decimating the enemy every single time! Believe it or not, we were able to make those planes so they were quite accurate at hitting a target.

The Christoff attic, or at least the roof over it, served another purpose in our lives as well. In winter, we'd take our sleds and climb the snow banks on the outside of the house, all the way up to the peak of the roof. Then we'd slide down and across the porch roof all the way to the ground. It was a mighty steep angle and we got some good speed.

That's how much snow there was in Crested Butte back then, year after year. My God, we got a lot of snow. And you know I can't remember any of the roofs, which sure weren't built with today's standards, caving in from the weight of the snow.

The years of the war dragged on, and for the most part the Spaghetti Gang went about our business, playing in attics, in the snow, and any other nonsense around town we could come up with.

We played war with my cousin Jimmy Christoff's train set in the big attic of 205 Maroon Avenue. Crested Butte, 2016.

An Odd Place to Play

Coke ovens just across the tracks from our house. National Park Service.

One thing I liked to do when I was alone and a little bored, was explore the old dome-shaped coke ovens across White Rock and over the railroad tracks. The purpose of the coke ovens was to heat the coal from the mine, super-heating it so the bituminous coal would turn to "coke," which was then sent on to Pueblo and used for steelmaking. When the ovens weren't being used I'd go in and out and on top of them, just goofing around, as a little kid does. When I think of what happened to Jewish people during that time period, I realize what a strange place this was for me to play.

Taking it Out on the Swallows

Toward the end of the war, my buddy Frank Bruno and I helped Sid Niccoli put up his hay. On days when the haying was rained out, Frank and I sometimes played with our BB guns, and the memory of what we did gives me haunting thoughts.

In those days, we had droves of swallows in the valley and on every ranch. The swallows built their mud nests under every eave and made big messes of droppings around the house and barn. With our BB guns, Frank and I would sit on the porch, take aim, and shoot any swallows perched on the electric lines that led from the shop to the house. We were good shots and killed more swallows than I care to remember.

Now, at this stage of my life, I look forward to seeing the swallows in the spring. When I think about why those pesky swallows are not coming back in the numbers they used to, I remember the way we shot so many of them without a second thought.

Looking back, it seems so heartless of us. I wonder why it didn't bother me then. Did growing up during the war make it more acceptable to hunt and kill animals like we did? Or is killing simply part of the human DNA?

I'll never know the answers to those questions, but I do know what a horrible spirit the war cast on that little town. I'd walk the streets and go by all those houses with stars, and young as I was, ten, twelve years old, I knew it was a terrible thing. The experiences of those years have resonated my whole life. –/–

Chapter 13

All About the Meat

Uncle Tom Sneller was blind in one eye but a heckuva shot. 1950s.

Green Behind the Ears

As soon as I was old enough, I graduated from BB guns to rifles and began hunting for big game. All the men in the family hunted, and I remember some of my early hunts as if they were yesterday.

One Sunday, Christy and I took off for the Red Hills (northeast of Gothic) to hunt elk. We picked our spot, an opening on the ridge looking across the valley. Pretty soon we spotted several elk coming down the other side. They stopped in a small bunch of quakies. Just right. I started shooting fast and furious. I wasn't hitting a damn thing.

All the men in my family hunted. Uncle Paul and Uncle Charlie packing out meat on horses. Crested Butte, 1950s.

Hunting was a way of life. My uncle George Sneller is on the right in this late 1920s or 1930s photo. Crested Butte.

Christy hollered, "You're shooting too high. Hold down. Hold down!" he said.

So, I did. Nothing.

By that time, the elk were as confused as we were and started milling in a circle, which they sometimes do. I stopped shooting and Christy said, "Quick, check your sights." Sure enough, when I looked, the sight had gotten moved to the top notch, probably when I stuck my gun in the scabbard earlier. I remedied the situation and after that hit two nice bulls. We tracked them down and both were dead.

Christy and I were, as they say, pretty green behind the ears but we proceeded to dress the elk out.

The elk were too far away and heavy for two kids to pack them out that night so we went back and told the older men, who decided that the next day while Christy and I were in school, they'd hire Rudy Malensek to haul our elk out with a team and a wagon.

When I got home from school that day, I got the bad news that Christy and I hadn't gotten the windpipes out of the elk and hadn't propped the carcasses open enough to dry out in the warm weather. All the meat on those two elk was spoiled, which upset me a good deal. Experience is a helluva teacher, though, and I never made that mistake again. That was a bitter lesson.

A Good Hunt, No Meat

Our disastrous hunt didn't deter Christy and me, and quite often we went up to the Red Hills to hunt. Long before I was old enough to join them, the Christoffs had built a stone hut out of those flat shale rocks you find up in the Red Hills. The hut was about four feet by four feet, big enough for two of us to sit in. It was three sided, with the rockslide hill making up the back wall. The walls were a good four or five feet high, without a roof of course, and there were a couple benches just the right height so you could see out of the openings they'd left to shoot from. There were some quakies on one side and on the other side there was a little stream. Deer traveling back and forth crossed in front of the hut—if you were lucky.

One day Christy and I hiked up to the hut and sat all day long on those nice flat benches, waiting for some game to cross in front of us on the way to water at the nearby creek.

The hut was a several hour walk from the where our folks had dropped us off, but the Christoffs were walkers! They never shied away from a long walk, and as a matter of fact I don't remember them ever having horses.

One day Christy and I hiked up to the hut and sat all day long on those nice flat benches, waiting for some game to cross in front of us on the way to water at the nearby creek. The benches were out of the wind, we had plenty of water, and a lot to eat. We were comfortable and the view was majestic. I don't know what we did to make the time pass, but probably we did a lot of talking. Christy was not the type to smoke, drink, or get into any of that nonsense.

We didn't have any luck that day but I remember it as one of the more enjoyable hunts of my life.

Too Mesmerized to Shoot

I was still young and inexperienced when Uncle Tony, Christy's dad, took us, along with Jimmy, hunting up toward Gothic, far to the west of the Christoff hut. We hiked into a big draw when all of the sudden a few dozen head of elk came down a ridge off the hill to our left. They headed straight toward us, galloping down that snowy hill single file. Jimmy started shooting first, as soon as they came in range. Me—I was too mesmerized by the sight of the elk to think of firing. Jimmy was shooting to beat the band and the rest of us just let him shoot, thinking he was gonna take one down pretty quick but nothing was happening. He emptied his gun and turned to me and said, "Hand me your gun," and I did. I guess he figured he didn't have time to reload his own rifle. After several more shots he finally had one down, which was enough for us to carry out. Christy and I had already learned our lesson about how much meat a person can handle.

I went on a lot of hunts with the Christoff side of the family, but the only photo I have of us together is at a pig roast in the 1940s. Left to right, Pauline Guerrieri, Aunt Donna Sneller Christoff, unknown, Kathy Christoff, Jimmy Christoff, Paul Guerrieri, Jimmy Christoff's wife, me, Lucille Guerrieri, unknown, "Christy" Christoff, Ernest Guerrieri, Uncle Tony Christoff.

Double Top

I was with the Christoffs another time hunting on the low end of Double Top Mountain. All day long we hunted and didn't seen a darn thing. Along about dusk, Jimmy and I walked up a ridge to our left and saw two bull elk halfway up the hill, headed down to the stream to get a drink.

"Go to the right. I'll head left," Jimmy said.

Well, I started down through the quakies and walked maybe a hundred yards. There stood the elk, stopped, grazing. I moved from one tree to another, trying to get an open shot but I spooked them and they threw their heads up. I swear they were so close together, and their movements so synchronized, they looked like their antlers were tied together. What a sight! They trotted off a small distance and stopped. I got off a perfect shot, killed one bull and cut his throat, then walked out to get help.

It was dark by the time I found Jimmy and the crew. "I killed one of those bulls," I told them, and we started out with flashlights, back through the quakies. We walked back and forth and around and around, trying to find my elk. I hadn't been smart enough to hang something from a tree to mark the spot, like my hat or a coat or something.

After a good long time my uncle Tony started getting upset. "Are you sure you killed him?" he kept asking. He was pretty perturbed.

I kept saying, "Yeah, I'm sure," but even I was beginning to wonder if we'd ever find that elk.

At last we found him and it was a nice six-point bull. We dressed him out and brought out all four quarters, leaving the horns behind. In those days, the horns weren't important because hunting was all about the meat. Even if we'd brought out that nice rack it would've ended up in the Crested Butte dumps.

An Uncanny Shot

All my uncles were hunters, but Uncle Tom had a remarkable ability with a gun, which was on full display one year at a 4th of July picnic at Uncle Charlie's place up Brush Creek. Below the house some two or three hundred yards were some old cars and a bunch of junk. A few of us wandered down there with Uncle Tom, who had a twenty-two rifle with him. We took turns picking up cans or pieces of metal and throwing them up in the air for Uncle Tom to shoot. He hit them every darn time. Every time, which was pretty impressive but nothing compared to what came next.

Uncle Tom hunted his whole life. Photo taken around 1919. Crested Butte.

My cousin, Gus Veltri, picked up an old windshield blade, held it up, and we all looked at Uncle Tom.

"Throw it in the air," he said.

I figured there was no way he'd hit it but sure enough. Bang! He blasted that

One of the hunting groups up Brush Creek, 1950s. Uncle Charlie Guerrieri is on the horse. Uncle Paul Guerrieri is second from left. I hired on as a hunting guide only once. Once was enough!

narrow blade in two with his shot. I was dumbstruck and bug-eyed but Gus had some wherewithal. "How the heck did you do that?" Gus said.

"Shoot when it's at its highest point, just before it starts down," Uncle Tom said, and turned away to join the other adults up the hill.

Well, I've tried to do just that a million times, but never with the success of Uncle Tom. Even today, it's hard for me to believe he had that kind of timing and aim, especially considering he only had one eye due to an accident with a gun he had when he was a kid.

Another example of his hunting prowess came years later. A bunch of us left early in the morning from Uncle Paul's cabin on Brush Creek to hunt deer. We took off on horseback, crossed the East River Bridge, went up the road and turned right at the Veltri house. From there we headed up Strand Hill, single file. There was snow on the ground, and to the right of us, about 100 yards or so, was a stand of quakies.

Two deer bounded out. Every one of us saw them, but Uncle Tom, who was one horse ahead of me, was out of his saddle, had his gun out of his scabbard, and was kneeling to shoot before any of the rest of us even moved.

He put his sights on the deer and hollered, "Do you want 'em? Do you want 'em?" Someone said "No," because sometimes a hunting party wants to wait for a bigger buck. Uncle Tom held off, but there's no doubt in my mind he could've shot those deer, no problem, before the rest of us were out of our saddles. He was unreal.

Big Nora Saves the Day

Of all my uncles, the one least interested in hunting was Uncle Jim. His horse, Nora, however, was in great demand as a hunting horse. One year Vic Niccoli was lucky enough to borrow Nora during hunting season.

Vic hunted above Sid's upper place, and a big bull elk came within range. He jumped off Nora, trained his sights on the elk, and took a shot. The elk went down, hard, and Vic started walking toward it. Figuring the elk was dead, he lumbered along, closer and closer to the carcass, further and further from Nora. As he got close to the elk, without warning, it jumped up and charged at him. Vic turned, scared to death, wondering how in the world he'd outrun that elk and get back to Nora. He hadn't taken three strides when he saw that good ol' horse just yards away. Unbeknownst to him, as he walked toward the downed elk Nora had followed behind him. He jumped on and took off fast, thanking his lucky stars.

The story doesn't end there, and the rest doesn't sound probable to me. As legends do, this one may have gotten enhanced in the telling, but I was told many times over that as Vic galloped away on Nora he turned around in the saddle, took a lucky shot, and killed the injured elk. Can you imagine a man riding full tilt to get away from a charging bull elk and at the same time getting a shot off with a rifle?

Whether that part of the story is true or not, the elk did die and its horns were mounted and hung in Sid's upper place. The horns are a lot bigger set than the set we've got hanging in our house. I know because I got to see them a few years after Vic shot the elk. I'll never forget seeing them, or the unpleasant experience I had at the time, which leads me to another story.

Things seemed to be settled down come morning, but one of the hunters from the fight refused to go on the hunt because he was sure the other guy was gonna shoot him.

I'd hired on with Frankie Guerrieri to guide some out-of-town hunters, and we used Sid's place as a base camp. The night before the hunt, in the same room where the horns were hung, the hunters were drinking galore, probably whisky, which was popular back then. As things go when people drink, the hunters started to get pretty rowdy. Their conversation got louder and louder, and a slight disagreement turned into a shouting match in the blink of an eye.

Even though I was young, I'd seen enough fights to know this wouldn't end well. I didn't want any part of it.

I walked outside to wait it out, but it was late October and after a time I got cold. Hoping they'd resolved their problems, I started to go back in. I walked through the first door on the screen porch and was just starting to open the main door when one of the drunks stormed out, throwing the door open and plastering me into the opposite wall. I didn't say a word even though I was a little banged up. I just headed to my bunk.

Things seemed to be settled down come morning, but one of the hunters from the fight refused to go on the hunt because he was sure the other guy was gonna shoot him. After much back and forth and some cajoling, we got past that problem. The six hunters plus me and Frankie saddled up and started up the trail.

What a bunch of whiners those hunters turned out to be. I was the low man on the totem pole and every time a hunter complained of his stirrups being too long or too short or a saddle pad slipping, or any other damn thing, Frankie said, "Rich, go help that guy out."

What a nightmare. If being a hunting guide meant putting up with drinking, fighting, and whining, I wanted nothing to do with it. I left that evening and never worked as a guide again.

A Bear in a Tree

Bear hunt on Crested Butte Mountain. Left to right, Bill Guerrieri, Gaspar "Muzzy" Guerrieri, Jim Moore, Paul Guerrieri. 1950s.

Around the time of my brief career as a hunting guide, Uncle Paul was having a tough time keeping his cows on his grazing permit on Crested Butte Mountain because a bear up there was scaring the cows back down the hill. Day after day Uncle Paul drove those cattle up to the range and the next day they'd be back at the low fence.

Well, a fellow named Pecharich who had hound dogs offered to help get that bear. Always up for a hunt, Uncle Paul and a bunch of my other relatives joined Pecharich and off they went. Pecharich had a tight hold of them dogs until they caught the bear's scent. Then he let 'em go and it didn't take long before the bear was up a tree, an easy shot.

I guess it was an exciting moment, because there are several photos in the family albums of the bear hunt. Killing a bear that scares cattle wouldn't be a normal thing to do nowadays, but I guess the people of Crested Butte were rather primitive when it came to treatment of wildlife. If wild animals were a nuisance or could provide us with meat, we killed them, but that's the way our culture was in them days.

Along that line was an annual activity that would be considered cruel in today's world. In the spring when the groundhogs had their babies, the guys would go shoot them and the town would have a whistle-pig barbecue, which is what we called groundhogs. My cousin Sonny says baby whistle-pigs taste just like rabbit, though most people nowadays don't even know what rabbit tastes like either. –/–

Chapter 14

From Coal to Cattle

Aubrey Spann and his girls about the time I first met my wife, Phyllis, around 1940.
From left, Phyllis, Aubrey, Gerrie Lou, Audrey.

Chasing Pennies

WE MOVED AROUND A LOT IN MY CHILDHOOD AS MY FOLKS tried to make ends meet and get ahead. In their lifetimes, they went from pillar to post, and to hell and back to chase a penny. Dad almost always worked two jobs, plus any odd job that came to him.

While others sat back and let the world go by, my dad hustled to make another dollar. Maybe those other folks were more satisfied with their situation in life, while Dad was always thinking of the next thing to do.

If he got a little extra money and thought he could turn a profit he'd lease a ranch, run a few cows, and put up some hay. He was talented at buying and selling cattle, in part because he was able look at a cow and tell pretty darn close to what it weighed.

I remember one time he leased a place just south of Crested Butte, and one day a neighbor rancher named Aubrey Spann came by when Dad and I were working on that ranch. Aubrey had his three daughters with him, and I realize now that it was the first time I ever saw Phyllis Spann, who eventually became my wife. The men didn't talk long, so it wasn't much of an introduction for me and Phyllis.

My cousin "Sonny," younger than me, helped on Phyllis' and my ranch and has been a good friend. 1940s.

Later on, when he had enough money, Dad began to buy instead of lease ranches. He never kept the ranches long, selling them whenever he could turn a profit. I don't believe he went into those endeavors because he had a goal of being a rancher; he was taking a gamble being able to make a buck. His risk-taking must have paid off because otherwise my ma and him would've had a set-to about him losing money. She would have gotten after him, no doubt. And that I would have remembered!

Even though Dad was always out to get money, he was also generous, to a fault. One time in his later years, when Mom was working at Goad's Restaurant in Gunnison, which was down there where the Safeway is now, Dad dropped Mom off at work and saw a young fellow standing there on Highway 50 just a-shivering in the cold, miserable weather. Dad stopped and brought the guy to Goad's, bought him a meal, and literally gave the fellow the new coat off his back. He and the young man talked and the man agreed to work a little for Dad. They were supposed to meet again at Goad's the next day for work and so the kid could return the coat, but of course that fellow never showed up. My dad, without resentment, said, "He needed the coat worse than I did," and that was that.

Mom didn't always like him funneling money out to help other people, which Dad was always doing, mostly to family members who were down on their luck. Mom and Dad argued about it on a regular basis, but Dad just kept on giving.

Uncle Jim Guerrieri would always lend a hand. Gunnison, 1970s.

I guess generosity runs in the family. Dad's brother, Uncle Jim, was both a regular recipient of Dad's help and also the kind of guy who would always lend a hand. He'd work for free, "just to help out." He'd never accept a penny for pay—even though his own kids were growing up poor as church mice and had a tough life. They all turned out to be fine people, in spite of a childhood of hardship.

After I got married, two of Uncle Jim and Aunt Mary's sons, Vic and Angelo "Sonny" Guerrieri, helped Phyllis and I out on the ranch for years. Sonny and Vic are younger than me, and I remember one time after our three boys were born, we had pigs around the ranch here and I heard the damnedest noise coming from down in the corral. I went to see what was going on. There were my boys with Vic and Sonny, taking turns trying to rope those pigs, all of 'em laughing like hyenas. The way they carried on, Sonny and Vic included, you'd have thought they were a bunch of teenagers.

We had family get-togethers up Brush Creek at Uncle Charlie's ranch and at his hunting camp. Standing in front of the Old Comfort bunkhouse left to right, Charlie and Mary (Veltri) Guerrieri, Josephine Krizmanich, the others standing unknown. Sitting left to right, Kathryn Sneller Guerrieri, Bill Guerrieri, Paul Guerrieri, three unknown, George Krizmanich, 1950s. The hunting camp is still owned by Uncle Charlie's descendants.

Uncle Charlie's Place

By the early 1940s the Crested Butte coal mines began to wane. My dad and Uncle Charlie and Uncle Paul had all dabbled in ranching while they were still at the mine.

Early on, Uncle Charlie bought a ranch up Brush Creek, and we'd go visit him up there. It was quite a trip in those days, with the negligible road upkeep back then.

On the way to his place we'd stop to get a drink at an abandoned ranch house on the left, which had a free-flowing spring coming out of the mountain. A little ways after that, we turned right, traveled through the sage probably a mile to a rather steep incline leading to a rickety bridge. Another half mile, and we'd reach Uncle Charlie's ranch.

He had a huge log barn, a nice log house, and a small bunkhouse. I stayed in the bunkhouse with my cousin Ernest "Swede" Guerrieri one summer, working for Uncle Charlie. Living conditions in the bunkhouse were minimal, but the big house had a nice screened in porch, a small kitchen and living room, but a spacious front room.

We spent a good amount of time up there, even in winter. Oftentimes in winter, the folks would be at Uncle Charlie's and decide we all needed to go visit Sid Niccoli and his family. The quickest way to get there was to hitch up a team to a feed sled and take a shortcut over Farris Creek. This was safe only if the creek was frozen solid. Now, horses are pretty heavy, and as a kid I was always scared to death they'd break through the ice. I'd seen enough to know if that happened all hell would break loose, and we'd all be in danger. A short distance down the hill from Farris Creek came East River, a much bigger crossing, and I can still visualize those foreboding willow branches arched out over the river, and the horses stepping out on the frozen ice. I hung on for dear life every time, but I'm here to tell the tale, so obviously we made it across.

A little hill after the river crossing was a challenge, too, which at times the horses strained to manage, but it was the last obstacle. After that we'd head down through the flats, the horses pulling the sleigh with ease on to Sid and Justina's place on East River, where we always had a good visit with those fine people. Ranching was a good way of life compared to working in the mines, and suited the entrepreneurial spirit running in my family. After years of working for the bosses at the mine, my dad always said, "It's better to sell peanuts on the street and be independent than to work for somebody else."

It took quite a few years before ranching became a full-time occupation for any of the Guerrieris. During his years at the ranch up Brush Creek, Uncle Charlie still kept his job at the mine. He'd ride his horse two or three miles to the mine, leaving early morning before dawn in order to arrive on time. He and his wife, Mary Veltri Guerrieri, had eight children to raise. Uncle Charlie couldn't afford to be idle with that many mouths depending on him to keep them fed.

He was a conscientious worker, my uncle Charlie, and rarely missed work. On one odd occasion, he was headed to work on a foggy morning, and when he got to the Slate River Bridge his horse stopped and refused to go on. Ears trained forward, the horse stared ahead, at nothing at all. Charlie nudged the horse again. That horse

We did everything with horses back then. Some fellows with a plow and team at Uncle Charlie's place in the 1930s. Crested Butte.

wouldn't budge. Now Uncle Charlie was a solid individual, not prone to fanciful thinking, but when he next looked across that bridge he thought he saw an apparition, a white ghost hovering in the air. Surely the fog was playing tricks on him. He urged his horse forward, but no way that horse would budge. Finally, my fearless Uncle Charlie began to believe the ghost was real and maybe the horse knew something he didn't. He turned around and went home.

That's the only time I remember hearing of that generation in my family being late to work, so it stands out in my mind. They all had the immigrant spirit of striving to get ahead in America and one day get out of the mines and work for themselves. –/–

Talk about buck fever! I emptied my gun and didn't hit a darn thing. There were so many deer out there I didn't know where to shoot or which one to shoot at. I'm thinking most of my bullets went in the air. The deer scattered, and I didn't get a darn one of 'em.

Chapter 15

Lost Soul

I was proud of the nice buck I shot with Uncle Paul's .220 Swift rifle. Gunnison, 1945.

Getting By in Gunnison

When the mine began laying people off, my family packed it in and moved to Gunnison. I think it was the summer before my ninth grade—the entire move is a blur to me, and I'm not sure I really took in what it meant to be leaving my childhood town.

When we first got to Gunnison we lived in some cabins down by the Gunnison River where the nursing home is now. The cabins were pretty shabby, barely habitable, rundown affairs, which belonged to Uncle Paul and J.F. Ritter. "Cabins" was actually too fancy a name for them. Shacks would be more like it. We used one shack for sleeping and another for eating. At one time, they were rentals for summer tourists, but by the time we were living in them, they hadn't been used for some time and were dilapidated goddamn things.

We got by in those shacks for a while but come winter they were unsuitable. Then we moved into a house right behind the Rosemont Café on Main Street, which was

also owned by Uncle Paul and J.F. Ritter. For a time, Mom was the cook and Dad the bartender at the Rosemont. Dad also worked at filling the city stoker with coal to produce the electricity for the whole town of Gunnison. The other thing he spent a lot of time at was collecting scraps from restaurants and stores all over town to feed the pigs he owned. He'd fatten the pigs up and sell them. Anything for a buck, and it was a pretty good deal for him, getting all that free pig food.

I ate my meals at the Rosemont, but living behind it was not quiet. On weekends, what a crowd would show! Loud and boisterous. I remember the likes of Jim Moore, Ray Crandall, Art Stratman, Pete Moore, Joe Eccher, Ben Hall, and Buster Kunze showing up. They were all ranchers but many town people were there, too, and others I can't recall. Buster Kunze had a large family and his wife

Gunnison seemed sophisticated to a poor miner's kid like me. Gunnison News Champion, *around 1948.*

A loud, boisterous crowd at the Rosemont Café. Ranchers and townspeople showed up on weekends, but my uncle Paul made sure there were no fights. I recognize Jim Moore at the bar with the baseball cap and my cousin Ernest Guerrieri behind him, smiling. Gunnison, 1940s.

Playing basketball helped keep me out of too much trouble, I suppose. At 6'3" I was taller than most guys, earning me the nickname of "Legs" Guerrieri. Looks like I've got control of the jump ball in this Gunnison News Champion *photo, around 1948.*

was always with him. She was small as a mite and he was about six foot four. Pauline Moore, Pete's wife, once jokingly said that all Buster had to do was hang his pants on the bedpost and his wife would get pregnant. There were no fights at the Rosemont that I remember, just good fun.

Boxley took out his pistol and shot the tire of the kid's car, which didn't go over too big with the police department.

Some years later the restaurant was renamed The Vee Bar Seven. I remember a story about some rowdy son-of-a-buck kid that went in there and started a fight. My brother-in-law, John Boxley, a cop, got called in to take care of the situation. Boxley marched the kid out the door but the kid got away and started to drive off. Boxley took out his pistol and shot the tire of the kid's car, which didn't go over too big with the police department. I'm glad there wasn't that kind of excitement back when my mom and dad worked at the restaurant.

A Loner and a Smartass

In those early years in Gunnison I became kind of a loner and a smartass. Maybe I was trying to impress people or to have friends. I guess I was a backward child, coming from a little bitty old town like Crested Butte where I had good buddies and where I knew everybody. Old people, young people—I knew them all. Then I was thrown into big classes where I never felt like I fit in. The kids seemed more sophisticated than a miner's kid from Crested Butte.

I'd skip study hall to go play pool or some other nonsense because it was easy to pull the wool over Mrs. Rockwell's eyes. She was the librarian, in charge of study hall. We'd walk into the library, sign our names, and after a while slip out the door. She never paid much attention to whether we stayed or not.

Me, on the right, in my ornery high school days with my buddy Scott Gilmer. Gunnison, late 1940s.

In retrospect, it's a good thing my folks moved me to Gunnison because that's where I met Phyllis and made my way as a rancher, but at the time we moved I was a lost soul in a bigger town and a bigger school.

After a couple years, I began to get my feet under me, but it was too late to get much out of high school. The exceptions were the agriculture classes taught by a friend and teacher we called Doc Maurice. I don't know if he was a doctor or had a PhD or not, but he was a damn good teacher. He was the kind of teacher who tried to treat everybody as an individual, helping them out. He encouraged me, telling me I could learn something even though I didn't think I was capable. He gave me confidence when I had none.

After a couple years in high school, I began to get my feet under me. High school graduation photo. Gunnison, 1949.

In the latter part of high school we had to fill out a three-page questionnaire. What the questionnaire amounted to was a way for the teachers to find out your aptitude and interests. When they got through looking at my form, I went in to see the teachers and they said to me, "You don't have any interest in anything so there's nothing we can see that you'll succeed in." I don't know what I thought of that statement, but that sentiment was something I probably knew all the way along the line so I wasn't surprised. The thing about that questionnaire, though, was that it asked about scholastic stuff like history and English, but didn't measure my love of animals and aptitude in the ag classes. Also, I probably didn't give a damn when I was filling out the form.

Uncle Charlie and Buck Fever

After a stint of living in town, my dad and Uncle Charlie managed to buy the LaMoy place, a ranch near Parlin, ten miles or so east of Gunnison. We all moved out there, and I spent a good deal of time hunting with Uncle Charlie, which he loved more than ranching. In fact, when hunting season came, regardless of what needed to be done on the ranch, hunting came first and the ranch was secondary.

My dad would go on with his part of the ranch work, and whatever chores Charlie was supposed to be doing would still be waiting for him at the end of hunting season. Some things slipped through the cracks, I'm sure, but Dad and Uncle Charlie had been in business together before, and they'd come to an understanding. Theirs was a good partnership and worked well for the families, but it stamped in my mind how difficult it can be to share a business. Over my lifetime, Phyllis and I never went into business with anyone else, even though we had several opportunities.

While we lived in Parlin, Uncle Charlie shared his hunting passion with me. One day the two of us went out deer hunting on horseback, headed east toward the Parlin Flats. We rode for several hours without seeing anything. Then we topped a rise and there in front of us was a massive herd of deer. A hundred or more. We jumped off our horses and I got out my gun. "Shoot! Shoot!" said Uncle Charlie, urging me to hurry it up.

Talk about buck fever! I emptied my gun and didn't hit a darn thing. There were so many deer out there I didn't know where to shoot or which one to shoot at. I'm thinking most of my bullets went in the air. The deer scattered, and I didn't get a darn one of 'em.

We rode on, all day, and didn't see another deer. I imagine Uncle Charlie was pretty disgusted with my hunting prowess and disappointed that he let me do all the shooting.

Uncle Charlie Guerrieri's first love was hunting. Ernest "Swede" Guerrieri on right. Crested Butte, 1950s.

In spite of Uncle Charlie knowing what a poor shot I was, a few days later he rousted me out of bed one morning. "There are some deer across the creek and up the hill next to the cow shed. Get your gun and let's go," he said.

It didn't take but a minute for me to pull on my clothes and grab my gun. We took off, trying to sneak close enough for a shot. After a time, a doe funneled out by itself a little ways, about 100 yards away from us. "Shoot that one," he whispered to me. I took aim and darn if I didn't hit her. The shot was too far back for a kill, though, and she started off up the hill toward Tomichi Creek and Highway 50.

"Go after her," Uncle Charlie hollered at me, "Hurry up, by God, and get her before she gets near the highway."

I took off running, stopped every once in a while and fired my rifle. Every shot was a panicked one, so naturally I missed quite a few times. Eventually I found my mark and she finally fell down and died in some willows next to the creek, not even a quarter mile from the highway.

My uncle Charlie was a big man, fairly heavy, and he hadn't kept up with me at all. When he came laboring down the hill and saw how visible she was from the highway,

A bunch of deer up Parlin way, 1940s. I shot a big buck up in those cliffs on the left.

he said, "You go to the house and get on to school. I'll dress her out."

Like I say, we ate wild game year round, and we didn't need to be a spectacle.

During the time we lived in Parlin I also hunted up the LaMoy Draw many times. One time I walked up on the ridge and spooked a buck lying next to a small rock ledge. I took aim and downed it in one shot. It wasn't my first buck but was the first one I ever had with me in a picture.

At that time I hunted with a .220 Swift rifle I'd borrowed from my uncle Paul. What was good about that gun was it used a small shell and had a fast trajectory. The impact from the velocity of the bullet was enough to kill large game if you were accurate. But if you took a bad shot it would just wound the animal, which was terrible. I used that gun for several years until it was outlawed after the Colorado Game and Fish decided the caliber of the bullet caused too many injuries without kills.

I ended up buying my first rifle, a .270, from the sporting goods store owned by Uncle Paul and J.F. Ritter near the Rosemont Café. I used that gun to hunt with for twenty years or more. When my nephew, Gene Simillion, became a gun maker, he built me a beautiful custom gun and I handed the .270 down to my son Dexter.

The damnedest hunting sight I've ever seen was with Uncle Charlie in Lost Canyon. It was a few years after we left Parlin, and we'd driven as far as we could up the road, then rode our horses a good long way and tied them to some quakies. Uncle Charlie and I walked towards a draw he liked the looks of, each of us taking a different trail so we'd have distinct viewpoints. I was downwind from him a hundred yards or so when I heard a shot. I ran down the draw towards where I thought the shot came from and as I got closer, I heard the biggest racket going on down there. I came out into the open and there was Uncle Charlie shouting and laughing. He'd shot a buck and was trying to cut its throat. The deer was thrashing and lunging and Charlie was hanging on, yelling "I'm riding the sonofabitch. I'm riding the sonofabitch."

He was kinda draped over the deer, holding onto it, the deer half up and half down. That old man hanging onto that deer was an unforgettable sight.

We dressed the deer out and started walking out of the draw to get the horses. Uncle Charlie had a black horse with white spots named, not too creatively, Spot. Uncle hated walking and about every 100 yards or so he had to stop and rest, and each time he'd call out, "Come on, Spot. Come on, Spot," hoping against all odds that somehow Spot had untied himself from the quakie tree, heard Uncle's call, and was on his way to us. After a lot of walking and resting, we reached the horses, which were, of course, tied right where we'd left them.

We lived in Parlin until some guy from North Dakota who'd made a fortune up there on wheat offered more money for the ranch than Dad ever imagined it was worth.

By that time, a fellow by the name of Waterman was ready to sell his ranch in Gunnison. Waterman once owned the place in Crested Butte where Doug and Jan Washburn live now, and he and my dad were good friends. Waterman was a bronc rider and often won the contests down here at Cattlemen's Days. My dad once had a palomino mare named Pearl (see photo page 86) he kept up at Sid Niccoli's place, and that mare bucked everybody off who tried to break her. Dad begged and begged Waterman to ride her and take the buck out of her. Waterman had promised his wife he wouldn't ride any more broncs, so he said no, but Dad kept after him until he gave in. They saddled up that mare on top of a hill at Niccoli's and Waterman crawled on. She started bucking to beat hell, down off that hill, across the bridge and out in the meadow. Bucked and bucked, she did, but Waterman stayed on, and when Waterman got done riding her and walloping her, she never bucked another day in her life.

Anyway, after the sale of the Parlin ranch around 1940, Uncle Charlie and Dad struck a deal to buy Waterman's place on Lost Canyon Road in Gunnison. Little did I know at that time, having moved a dozen times or so during my short life, that I'd end up living on the Waterman ranch the rest of my life. –/–

Chapter 16

Life Lessons from Uncle Paul

Nowadays he would've been considered handicapped but Uncle Paul (right) was one of the toughest men I ever met. J.F. Ritter on the left. Gunnison, 1950s.

Kathryn and Paul Guerrieri. Gunnison, 1940s.

Don't Hesitate

FOR A TIME IN HIGH SCHOOL I LIVED with Uncle Paul and Aunt Kathryn at their ranch on the Gunnison River near where the nursing home is now. Living with him and Aunt Kathryn gave me a different view of the way people live.

Aunt Kathryn was a woman who never stopped cleaning her house. She kept it immaculate at all times. She cleaned so hard she had muscles in her arms like most men.

One bedtime evening, I went to ask her and Uncle Paul a question. They were in bed, propped up against some pillows. My uncle was smoking a cigarette attached to a long tube. The cigarette was on a table three or four feet away. A round cup affair held the cigarette and the tube was attached to it, making it so no ashes went in the bed! I'd never seen one of those kind of cigarette holders and I never saw one again. The fact that Aunt Kathryn let him smoke in her spotless house was a big deal, as was the vision of him looking like a king, a royal highness propped up in the bed like, smoking with that fancy tube and all.

Nowadays my uncle Paul would have been thought of as handicapped. When he was a small boy he was walking through the hay field and whoever was running the

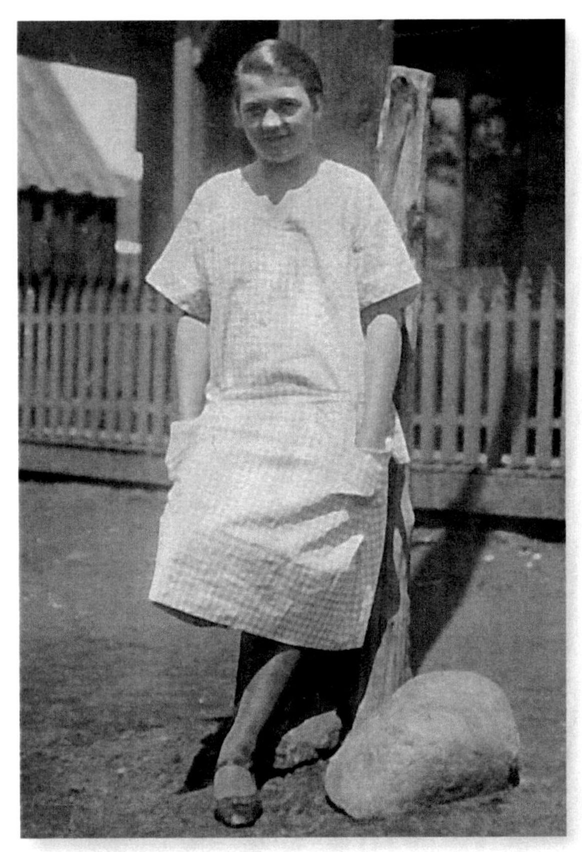

My aunt Kathryn had muscles in her arms as hard as a man's. White Rock Avenue, Crested Butte, 1930s.

mower didn't see him through the tall grass. The mowing sickle went right into his leg, cutting his ankle bone practically in two before the mower man could stop. For the rest of his life Uncle Paul walked with a limp and his ankle was twice the size of his opposite leg.

In spite of the accident, he grew into a muscular man who never backed down from anything. He was a go-for-it kind of guy in business, horseback riding, hunting, ranching, you name it.

He was also a fighter and a frequent visitor to the Elks Club. Uncle Paul would get to arguing with someone who would eventually invite him to go outside to continue the feud. I never heard of Uncle Paul losing a fight. One time he gave me this advice: "Listen, kid. When you're gonna fight, always be the first one out the door. Then as soon as the other guy gets over the threshold, don't hesitate. Hit 'em hard, right then, before they expect it."

Don't Toss the Pitchfork, Hold the Damn Reins

I helped Uncle Paul feed hay to his cows each morning with a team and sled before school. One time after we finished loading the sled full of hay, I climbed up and sat in the hay. He was on the ground and threw the fork up on top and struck me straight in the back! I just sat there too stunned in my mind to move. He shimmied up on the sled fast as soon as he realized what he'd done. He pulled the fork out and looked me over. Only one tine had stuck me, and it gave me a decent sized gash. There wasn't the thought to run to the doc as you might nowadays. He and Aunt Kathryn threw a little peroxide on it and a large bandaid and we called it good. The wound healed nicely, the experience more scary than serious.

Uncle Paul made a mistake that day with the fork, but not as bad as the one I made later while driving the team. He had a big, beautiful, blue roan mare he was training to pull. Bait, as she was called, was hitched up with an older horse. Now, the reason she was called Bait was because there was a fox farm on the opposite side of the Gunnison River from their ranch and anytime Uncle needed a workhorse, he'd wander over to the fox farm to see what was available. The horses at the fox farm were all slated to be butchered to feed the foxes, so they were not all that desirable, to say the least.

They were fine but the sled was a little beat up and needed repairs. My self-image, however, took a beating, especially after Uncle Paul read me the riot act.

Bait was doing pretty well in her training, and she was hitched up in a special way. The chain from the doubletree to the wagon was rigged so that green, inexperienced Bait couldn't pull the older horse out of whack.

When we were done with the feeding, I pulled the team up to Uncle Paul, who was waiting at the barn. "You go unhook 'em from the sled," he said.

With my team, Pearl and Scotch, years after I learned the hard way to always hold onto the lines. Son Dexter is on the sled with me. Gunnison, 1957.

Now, before I jumped down to go unhitch them, I threw each line on either side of the horses. The flopping of those lines spooked both horses and off they went, the poor sled bouncing and each bounce scaring the horses more. Lucky for me it wasn't too far to the fence at the end of the field, and the team stopped. Uncle and I ran over and settled them down. They were fine but the sled was a little beat up and needed repairs. My self-image, however, took a beating, especially after Uncle Paul read me the riot act. Oh, man, he was mad.

Never again in my life did I hitch or unhitch the wagon without holding both lines. I never tossed a pitchfork near anyone either. Life is a good teacher.

A Deer in the Back Seat

I'd drive my uncle Paul Guerrieri to Delta to buy beef even though I didn't have a license. He'd fall asleep, having bartended until two in the morning the night before. Gunnison, late 1940s.

Uncle Paul was still part owner of the Rosemont at that time, and the café bought live beef from the cattle auction yard down in Delta to butcher and serve. I often went with Uncle Paul on those beef-buying excursions. He had a gray Ford car and a 4x6 trailer he'd pull behind it. I didn't have my driver's license yet because I was too young but that didn't matter to Uncle Paul. A few miles out of town he'd pull over and say, "You drive."

He'd go straight to sleep while I drove. He was mighty tired, what with ranching during the day and staying up most nights in the café until the bar closed at two in the morning. I'd drive across the Sapinero bridge and over the winding damn road of Cerro Summit and Blue Mesa Pass. Then as we neared Montrose, I'd pull over and wake him up and he'd start driving again. The cops didn't patrol the highways so much back then so we weren't too worried outside of town. He'd take us on into Delta and after purchasing his beef, it was the same on the way home, as soon as we got outside of Montrose I'd take over the driving.

Kathryn and Paul Guerrieri. Gunnison, 1960s.

We'd take the beef back to the ranch where the family had built a small slaughterhouse for the purpose of providing meat for the cafe. Their slaughterhouse was very well thought out. The steer entered a walkway that had a heavy screen in front. Once the gate behind the animal was closed, someone walked around and shot the critter right in the head through the screen, then unfastened a side panel and the animal would roll down to a V shaped floor where it was real handy to skin and dress it out. A chain hoist and railing dropped the animal into a truck, which brought it over to the Rosemont cooler to age and later to be cut up for cooking and serving. A lot of customers came to the café just because of the fresh, good meat.

The wildest thing that ever happened on our way to Delta was during one of those times he told me to drive. We drove past what is now the dam and up the hill. A big semi truck passed us and a few minutes before we entered the big curve, we saw an injured deer, still kind of kicking, lying on the side of the road. The semi must've clipped the deer and just kept going. My uncle was a Johnny-on-the-spot kind of guy. He yelled for me to pull over and he jumped out and cut the deer's throat. We waited there a few minutes to let the deer bleed out. There were very few cars on the road at that time and no one went past while we were stopped there watching the deer bleed. We weren't pulling the little trailer on that trip, I don't know why not, so we opened the back door of the car, laid some old newspapers down on the floor and the back seat, and hoisted the deer in with us, his four feet sticking straight up. I jumped in the driver's seat with Uncle Paul in the back with the deer. He proceeded to dress out that deer, to some degree, as I drove along. Can you just picture a punk kid driving, four deer legs sticking up in the backseat, and my uncle back there wielding his knife? Oh, the looks we got from those few cars we passed. I was half terrified thinking we'd get pulled over.

To this day, I can't imagine how the bloodstains on our clothes must've looked to the people who saw us around town in Delta.

When we got to the other side of Cimarron I stopped in a place where there are some small scrub oaks. I watched to make sure there was no traffic coming and then we drug the deer out and up into the scrub oaks. We left it there until we finished our business in Delta that day. On the way home, we stopped and loaded the deer back in the car. To this day, I can't imagine how the bloodstains on our clothes must've looked to the people who saw us around town in Delta.

Years later, Uncle Paul got cancer and went to several doctors and had many operations. He rallied for some time and then slowly got worse. For one of his last doctor appointments in Montrose he asked me to drive him, which for me was reminiscent of those many trips we took together when I was a teenager. On the way to the doctor we drove down the curvy road and were almost to the halfway house when we saw a huge buck with a nice rack of antlers standing on the rock ledge. I stopped the car and we watched the buck for several minutes.

Not too long after that my uncle Paul passed away and I always thought seeing that buck at the end of his life was a wonderful tribute to a man who loved to hunt. The Lord works in mysterious ways. –/–

Chapter 17

Ranching for Good

I worked on the ranch from dawn to dark, so Phyllis raised the five kids almost single-handedly. Phyllis with two of our boys, Dexter and Burt, around 1960.

One Brick at a Time

THERE WERE TIMES IN THOSE EARLY YEARS OF MY LIFE that I thought I must have been born with a dent in part of my brain. My folks tried so hard to funnel me into learning something desirable. I rebelled at everything and must have had the word "No" imbedded in my DNA. My folks had other dreams for me, but I wanted to be outdoors, and I always preferred being with animals over book learning. Even in high school, instead of paying attention in class, I'd be staring out the window at Big John Wilson feeding his cattle with a team of horses, wishing I could be with him.

In retrospect, I was probably destined to become a rancher, and I was lucky my folks gave me the opportunity. When they bought the ranch from Waterman, they

We tried dairy farming before becoming full time ranchers. I showed one of our Herefords at Cattlemen's Days. Gunnison, 1952.

were planning to live there themselves. They started building themselves a house, but when Phyllis and I decided to get married, at ages 18 and 19, my folks sold us the ranch and we moved into the new house. They kept living in town and financed our purchase, since of course we had no credit.

Those early years of marriage, when we tried dairy farming and then started ranching, were tough. We kept having a hard time making payments and there came a time when we just couldn't do it. By then we had a couple kids, I was working sun-up to dark, and still struggling. My folks helped us out and that gave us a boost when we needed it most, and I'll always be grateful.

Dad working on one of his and Phyllis' schemes, bricking in the porch of our house. They were an unstoppable team. Gunnison, 1970s.

In the long run, we made a go at ranching, and in large part I believe this was because of my wife's love, positive outlook, and comfort with taking risks—which was something I was hesitant about. When you're in the ranching business, you have to not lose your nerve and to keep making improvements in the property and in the herd in spite of falling prices and bad weather.

Whenever there was an investment opportunity, Phyllis had boldness. She'd keep an eye out for ranchland at a bargain. Sometimes we succeeded, and she was the key.

She gave birth to five children and raised them almost single-handedly because I worked pretty much all the time. She had help from her folks and mine, which was a blessing.

Phyllis and my dad became the best of buddies. Dad, with his workaholic fierceness, and Phyllis with her ideas and perseverance, were an unstoppable pair. They knew no such word as "impossible." The projects they tore into—and I mean tore into, were something to behold. They poured cement, they built that damn porch, they tore down the dining room wall, built a yard for the kids to play in, bought the playhouse from Frankie Guerrieri that's still here and put the foundation under it, built a root cellar. Any idea that Phyllis had, my dad was one hundred and ten percent behind.

They didn't consult with me. Hell no. If they'd asked me I'd have said, "No. Things are fine the way they are." Instead, I'd come home from the field and not know what I'd find, like that one time the wall was coming down between the kitchen and the old porch, with kids hauling bricks out the door one at a time. It was a helluva mess at the time but, as usual, turned out to be a very good thing in the end.

With her as the inspiration, sometimes literally tearing down old walls and sometimes building new ones, we created a pretty good life for our family, a life I could never have imagined as a kid in Crested Butte.

A Cowboy and a Friend

Ranching became my life and I was lucky over the years to meet people along the way who prepared me for it. My dad and all my uncles, the ag teacher who encouraged me, and Phyllis' family who have ranched in the Gunnison valley since the 1880s. Her dad, Aubrey Spann, accepted me and taught me a tremendous amount about the ranching business. I spent an inordinate amount of time with him in those first few years, and I was with him the day I met another important man in my life, a man who would become a lifelong friend.

I was on a stack of hay and looked out toward Ohio Creek road to see a young tow-headed fellow come walking toward the stack. When the young man got close, Aubrey, not one to beat about the bush, said, "Are you here hunting for work?"

The man pointed at a pitchfork sticking in the ground and said, "I know how to handle that pitch fork."

Aubrey put him to work on the stack that very minute and I worked alongside him the rest of haying season. His name was Steve Christensen and we became good friends for the next twenty or more years.

Steve worked for Aubrey for about a year or so and lived in the Spann bunkhouse. You can still see the bunkhouse, which sits close to Highway 135. One day Steve came to eat with us, driving Aubrey's Jeep with the canvas on top and those old plastic windows. Steve was a young man trying to make ends meet, and I had an elk tag, not filled. After noontime dinner, he and I decided to take a trip up the Lost Canyon. I grabbed my gun and off we went. We drove to the top of the hill on the Lost Canyon road and turned left, following an old dirt road. After a mile or so we came out in a small park. A bull elk stood opposite us just this side of a ridge. We debated for a few seconds because the elk's color was more white than tan, an old elk. "The meat might be tough," I said.

"Or maybe not," Steve said.

I've never met anyone as fearless as my good friend Steve Christensen. Gunnison, 1960s.

Steve introduced me to the sport of team roping. I'm on one of my favorite rope horses, Lolly, in a team roping competition at the Gunnison County Fairgrounds, 1970s.

In the end, I shot that bull.

We dressed him out and cut the head off and left it. It had a nice six point spread but we left the horns. We only wanted the meat, and we loaded that big bull in the Jeep. It was almost dark by then and we drove out with our lights on. The heat of the fresh elk steamed up the windows so much that Steve had to turn on the defrosters. About that time, we turned off the Lost Canyon road and headed for Highway 135 and down to the bunkhouse.

Steve butchered the animal and tried to eat the meat but it was so tough he couldn't chew it, like leather. He gave it to the dogs and they barely could chew it either.

A few years later he and I tried to find that nice set of horns but we never could.

After working for Aubrey all fall, Steve went to working for Big John Wilson. A few months later, about midnight, we heard a banging on our back door. I opened the door and there was Steve. "I've got an elk in the back of my truck," he said.

We unloaded the elk into the shed nearest to the house, and Steve told the story of how that elk came to be in his truck. Apparently a local rancher had gotten plumb out of sorts because whenever he'd feed his cows, here would come a herd of elk and eat up all the hay. Earlier that day when the elk were across the creek and on a hillside, the rancher started shooting. He killed a good number, then called several buddies and told them to hurry come get an elk. How Steve learned about it I am not sure but according to him, once they had the elk loaded up in various trucks, there was a pretty big patch of red where the blood stained the snow. The rancher got a little panicky, so they all saddled up and drove the cattle up the hill, down the hill, chasing them back and forth, around and around, to obliterate the signs of blood. Think about that for a minute. Just picture the cowboys and cows trying to stomp out evidence in the dark of night.

We cut up Steve's meat in the wee hours, while all our kids were asleep. We tried to be quiet, but I found out years later that at least one of our sons was well aware of what we did, but knew enough not to say anything. I never heard talk around town of those elk being killed, either.

Steve was a cowboy, a horseman, and I never saw anyone since him that was as fearless. One time he was on a horse of ours named Geronimo and he tried to rope a bear from horseback. Thank heavens he missed!

He'd ride any horse and knowing he was a bronc-rider, folks would give him rank horses to break. One time on that alkali flat of Harrises over the hill from our Mill Creek cabin, a mare he was riding started bucking to beat the band. I didn't see that little rodeo but when he came over the hill to where I was, I looked over at him and he was as white as a ghost, not from fear, but from all the alkali the horse kicked up.

I hardly knew how to swing a rope before I met Steve, and he was the one who taught my boys and me to love the sport of team roping and calf roping. He had a horse named Rabbit, and he built a little catch pen at the end of our corral lane to practice. One time he roped a calf, threw his slack, and somehow the rope wrapped around Steve's neck. Good thing the lane was short and the calf had to stop or Steve would've been choked by that rope.

Imagine looking down a half mile into the canyon with nothing but a small rope between you and certain death.

Steve was young when I met him, still getting his degree at Western State College. He took a job on the construction of the Blue Mesa dam. The job required being lowered with ropes down the side of the cliff where he'd a jackhammer to pound away at the rock. Imagine looking down a half mile into the canyon with nothing but a small rope between you and certain death. It was not a job for the faint of heart, and it was truly dangerous. Phyllis and I had a friend, a kid by the name of Hamilton, who got killed working for the reservoir.

Most times after work on the dam, Steve didn't have time to change clothes before his college classes. One time a professor took him aside and spoke to him after class, telling him his dirty clothes weren't appropriate. Steve explained the situation, and after that the professor figured anyone that dedicated to class was an okay fellow. Steve graduated with high marks and a business degree.

After Steve got married he moved to Montrose and worked for the Federal Land Bank and became the president of the bank. When the farm crisis hit, his bank had to foreclose on a lot of good farmers and ranchers. It bothered Steve a lot, to take the livelihood away from friends and neighbors.

I had many more experiences with Steve but I think I will close with this—after he left Gunnison I would call him every now and then, or he would call me. One morning he called me and wanted to recall our friendship, and we had a nice conversation. During the conversation, I didn't realize the kind of depression he was in. Hours later, I found out he took his life right after our call. What a waste to have a beautiful man go like that.

How Many Miles

Me in 1944, my last year in Crested Butte.

Sometimes, I think back on the day in seventh grade when our teacher, Rudy Sporcich, took a group of us students to the top of Crested Butte Mountain. We started out straight from the schoolhouse. There was no trail and we scrambled up the mountain from rock to rock. We climbed and climbed and I never thought we'd reach the top. Oh, what a sight we had when we did get there, our cozy little town down below, with us standing eye to eye with the tall mountains we'd looked up to all our lives!

We recorded our ascent by writing our names on tiny scraps of paper and putting them in an open-topped tin can we left between some rocks. Not many folks went up there back then, and of course there was no ski lift. It took us all day, and by the time we got back, I was proud, but just a-dragging.

Little did I know on that beautiful day that weeks later I'd leave Crested Butte and never live there again, that the Spaghetti Gang adventures were coming to a close, or that in the years that followed, almost everyone I knew would leave town. We'd climbed the mountain, written out our names, and with the naiveté of youth, we'd claimed our place. But change is inevitable. Now, I wonder how many miles the names in that tin can traveled in the wind before the paper disintegrated. –/–

The End

Crested Butte Mountain overlooking the town, 1950s. Photo by Robert W. Richardson.

Epilogue

My Town

Richard Guerrieri with Cara Guerrieri

Do you see the sphinx of a mountain rising high with its crags, gullies,
Its pristine elegance watching down on what once was my town.
Do you know it once saw me, born in a gray house,
Saw me playing marbles in the dirt streets,
Swimming with buddies in little old Coal Creek.

Did you ever see the puff, puff of the locomotive pulling its cars,
Stopping at the water tower, steam hissing from its bowels.
Did you smell the dust and hear the noise
As black gold was loaded into large railroad cars,
Or hear the steel wheels screeching, whining, spitting out sparks,
Moving forward, faster, faster as another load of coal rumbled away.
This was my town.

Did you know that Mondays were for washing whites
Because the air was cleaner that day, less coal dust and smoke.
Tough women in aprons hung every line, pulley to pulley with clothes
Waving in the breeze like the surf of a sea,
Fluttering across town from outside every house.

Have you felt the rumbling of the railroad cars,
When the big half-moon coupler on one car clacks,
Hitches itself to the receiving end on another,
The noise vibrating down the line car to car until the sound dies off while
A man on the ladder inspects each hookup.
Music in a different chord.
This was my town.

Did you know the miners, the poor immigrants
Enduring back-breaking hard work,
Earning shelter and food for their families,
Men who lived the saying, *owed my soul to the company store,*
And worried each day, *did I load enough coal to pay my bill.*
I knew them. They were my dad and grandpas and uncles.

Can you remember that come evening, this used to be a quiet town,
Patriotic to the core, sending sons and daughters to war.
Quiet and dark, except for the mine's night watchman
The glow of his lantern bobbing as he walked
Up and down next to the railroad cars, keeping the company's cargo safe.
Did you see his light between the gaps of houses,
As if his lantern went on, off, on, off.

I know he saw what I saw, someone, a friend perhaps,
Down on his luck, climbing a railroad car ladder,
Throwing chunks of coal to the ground,
Stealing two or maybe three gunnysacks full
Just to keep the family warm a few more frigid nights.
The watchman's lantern kept moving in the other direction,
Compelled by a compassion that trumped company rules.
This was my town.

Did you ever climb Crested Butte Mountain,
Back when there was no trail to speak of.
It was an arduous scramble for a boy like me.
Now I ride to the top, look down and wonder
Who would I be if not for the extraction of black gold
Which formed my small slice of town heaven.

Did you know about the families that left, like mine,
Ripped away by the slow death and shallow grave of coal.
Progress in the eye of the beholder,
But not to me as a boy who no longer had a place here.

I am old now, an old man, and I reflect on these things,
Jealously hanging on to recollections of a town I once knew.
Now it is time for those memories to fade.
Now I am gone, but the mountain, in splendor, remains,
Still watching, still eyeing all.

Family Tree

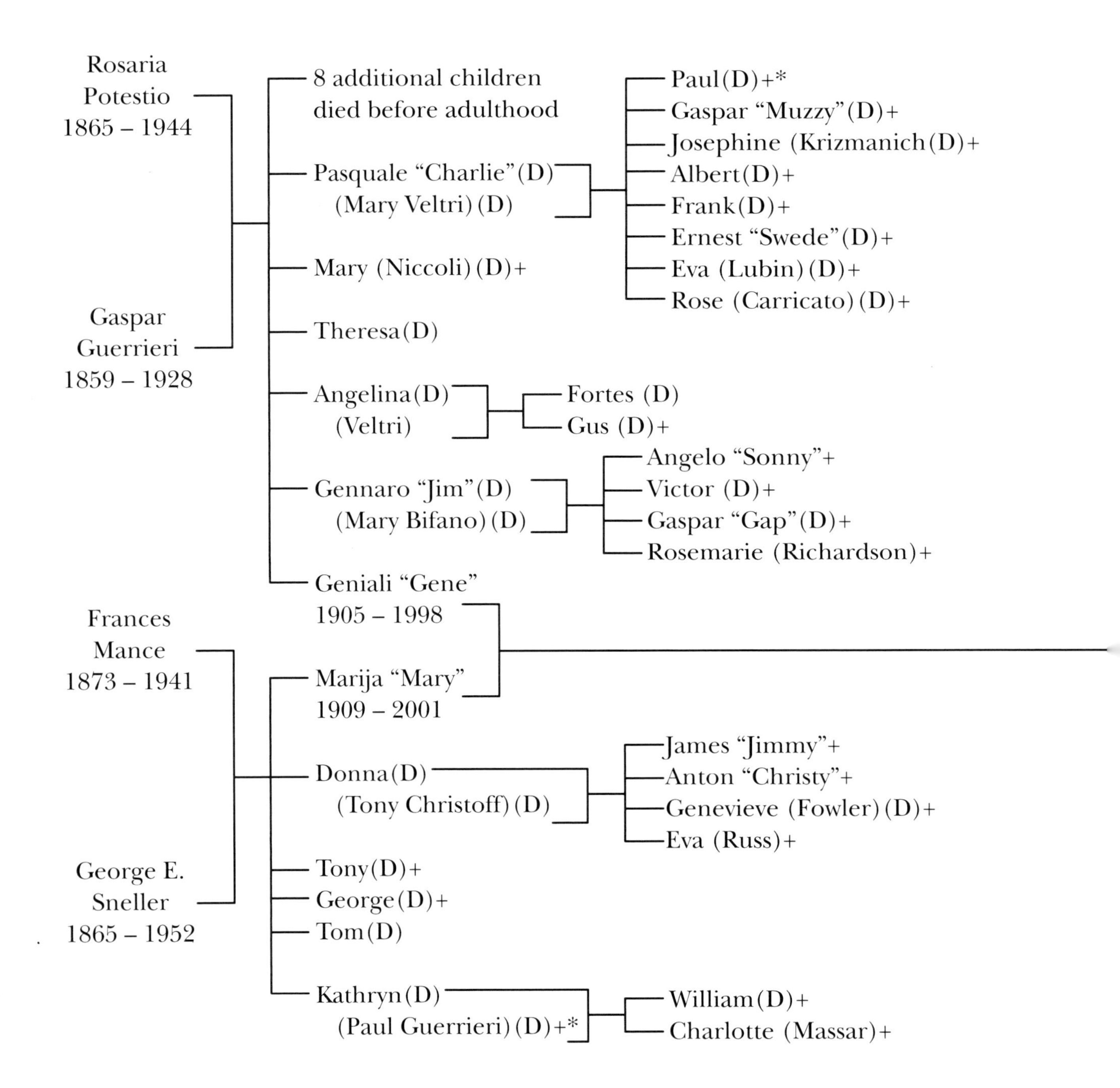
Rosaria
Potestio
1865 – 1944
Gaspar
Guerrieri
1859 – 1928
8 additional children
died before adulthood
Pasquale "Charlie" (D)
(Mary Veltri) (D)
Mary (Niccoli) (D)+
Theresa (D)
Angelina (D)
(Veltri)
Gennaro "Jim" (D)
(Mary Bifano) (D)
Geniali "Gene"
1905 – 1998
Paul (D)+*
Gaspar "Muzzy" (D)+
Josephine (Krizmanich (D)+
Albert (D)+
Frank (D)+
Ernest "Swede" (D)+
Eva (Lubin) (D)+
Rose (Carricato) (D)+
Fortes (D)
Gus (D)+
Angelo "Sonny"+
Victor (D)+
Gaspar "Gap" (D)+
Rosemarie (Richardson)+
Frances
Mance
1873 – 1941
George E.
Sneller
1865 – 1952
Marija "Mary"
1909 – 2001
Donna (D)
(Tony Christoff) (D)
Tony (D)+
George (D)+
Tom (D)
Kathryn (D)
(Paul Guerrieri) (D)+*
James "Jimmy"+
Anton "Christy"+
Genevieve (Fowler) (D)+
Eva (Russ)+
William (D)+
Charlotte (Massar)+

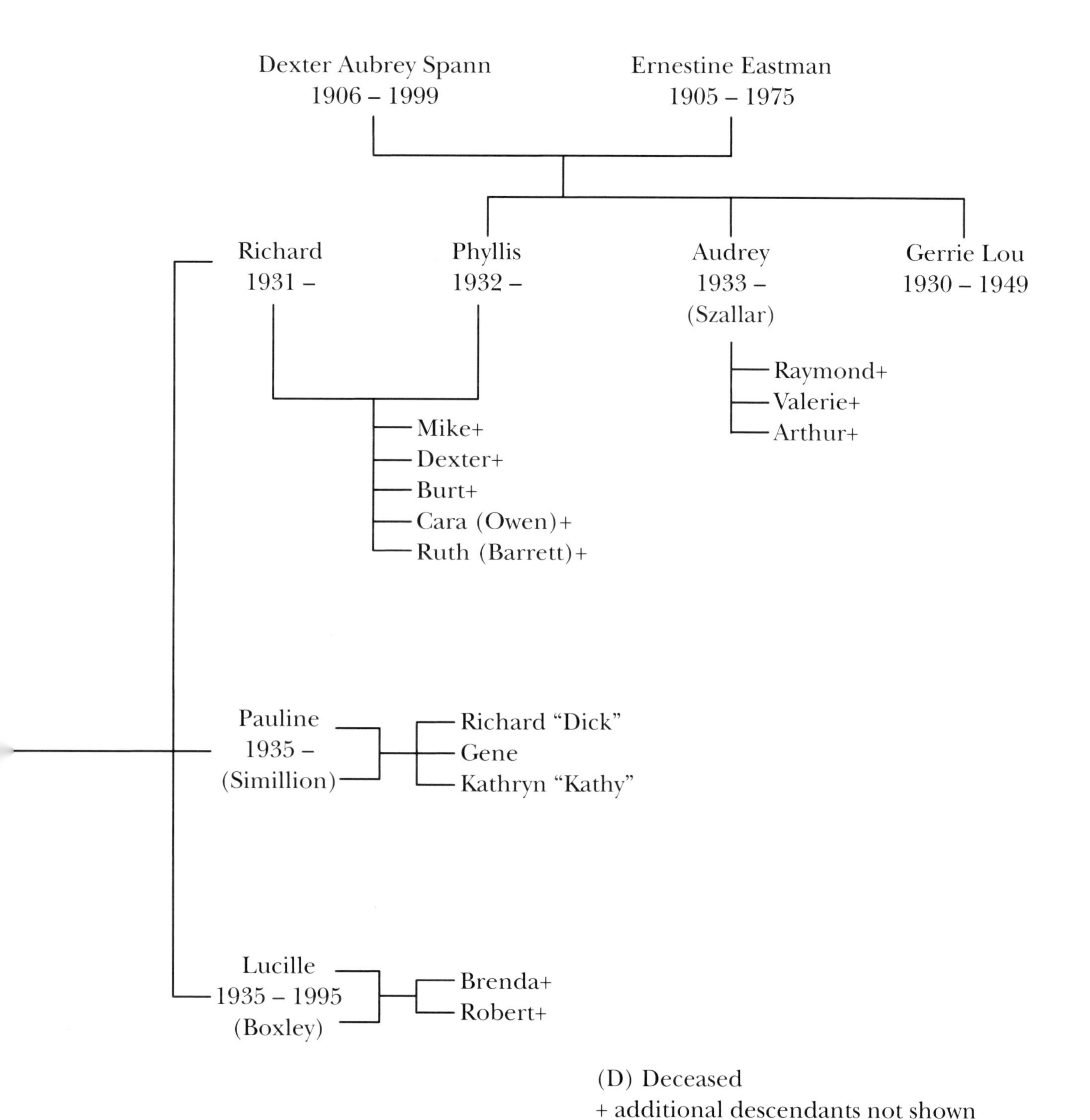

(D) Deceased
+ additional descendants not shown
* Paul Guerrieri appears in two places

Richard, age 86, editing The Spaghetti Gang *while watching for elk. Hunting camp, 2017. Gunnison.*

The Guerrieris, a family of storytellers. Supper at the ranch is often a storytelling bonanza, as one tale leads to another and another, for hours on end. Richard and Phyllis Guerrieri with their children, left to right, Burt, Dexter, Jane Ordway (Dexter's wife), Phyllis, Ruth, Richard, Mike, and Cara. Bar Slash Bar Ranch, Gunnison, 1980s.

About the Authors

Richard Guerrieri is a lifelong rancher who, as a friend said, "is also an amateur philosopher," traits that don't often go together. Now he adds "entertaining writer" to his list of assorted skills. Richard was born in 1931 in Crested Butte and has lived his entire life in Gunnison County.

Cara Guerrieri earned her Masters in Fine Arts in Creative Writing from Western State Colorado University. Her nonfiction stories can be found in the *Crested Butte Magazine* and *Gunnison Country Magazine*. She loves the magic of shaping fun and universal stories from life's jumble of experiences.